THE BRITISH REPUBLIC
1649–1660

British History in ~~Perspective~~
General Ed~~itor~~

PUBLIS~~HED~~

Rodney Barker *Politics* ~~People and Government~~
C. J. Bartlett *British Foreign* ~~Polic~~*y in the Twentieth Century*
Jeremy Black *Robert Walpole and the Nature of Politics*
in Early Eighteenth-Century Britain
Anne Curry *The Hundred Years War*
John W. Derry *British Politics in the Age of Fox, Pitt and Liverpool*
William Gibson *Church, State and Society, 1760–1850*
Brian Golding *Conquest and Colonisation: the Normans*
in Britain, 1066–1100
Steven Gunn *Early Tudor Government, 1485–1558*
Richard Harding *The Evolution of the Sailing Navy, 1509–1815*
Ann Hughes *The Causes of the English Civil War*
Ronald Hutton *The British Republic, 1649–1660*
Kevin Jefferys *The Labour Party since 1945*
D. M. Loades *The Mid-Tudor Crisis, 1545–1565*
Diarmaid MacCulloch *The Later Reformation in England, 1547–1603*
Keith Perry *British Politics and the American Revolution*
A. J. Pollard *The Wars of the Roses*
David Powell *British Politics and the Labour Question, 1868–1990*
Michael Prestwich *English Politics in the Thirteenth Century*
Richard Rex *Henry VIII and the English Reformation*
G. R. Searle *The Liberal Party: Triumph and Disintegration, 1886–1929*
Paul Seaward *The Restoration, 1660–1668*
Robert Stewart *Party and Politics, 1830–1852*
John W. Young *Britain and European Unity, 1945–92*

History of Ireland

D. G. Boyce *The Irish Question and British Politics, 1868–1986*

History of Scotland

Keith M. Brown *Kingdom or Province? Scotland and the Regal Union,*
1603–1715

History of Wales

A. D. Carr *Medieval Wales*
J. Gwynfor Jones *Early Modern Wales, c.1525–1640*

Please see overleaf for forthcoming titles

FORTHCOMING TITLES

John Belcham *Nineteenth-Century Radicalism*
Eugenio Biagini *Gladstone*
Peter Catterall *The Labour Party, 1918–1940*
Gregory Claeys *The French Revolution Debate in Britain*
Pauline Croft *James I*
Eveline Cruickshanks *The Glorious Revolution*
John Davis *British Politics, 1885–1931*
David Dean *Parliament and Politics in Elizabethan and Jacobean England, 1558–1614*
Susan Doran *English Foreign Policy in the Sixteenth Century*
David Eastwood *England, 1750–1850: Government and Community in the Provinces*
Colin Eldridge *The Victorians Overseas*
S. Fielding *Britain and the Impact of World War II*
Angus Hawkins *British Party Politics, 1852–1886*
H. S. Jones *Political Thought in Nineteenth-Century Britain*
D. E. Kennedy *The English Revolution, 1642–1649*
Anthony Milton *Church and Religion in England, 1603–1642*
R. C. Nash *English Foreign Trade and the World Economy, 1600–1800*
W. M. Ormrod *Political Life in England, 1300–1450*
Richard Ovendale *Anglo-American Relations in the Twentieth Century*
David Powell *The Edwardian Crisis: Britain, 1901–1914*
Robin Prior and Trevor Wilson *Britain and the Impact of World War I*
Brian Quintrell *Government and Politics in Early Stuart England*
Stephen Roberts *Governance in England and Wales, 1603–1688*
W. Stafford *John Stuart Mill*
Alan Sykes *The Radical Right in Britain*
Ann Williams *Kingship and Government in Pre-Conquest England*
Michael Young *Charles I*

History of Ireland

Toby Barnard *The Kingdom of Ireland, 1641–1740*
Sean Duffy *Ireland in the Middle Ages*
Alan Heesom *The Anglo-Irish Union, 1800–1922*
Hiram Morgan *Ireland in the Early Modern Periphery, 1534–1690*

History of Scotland

I. G. C. Hutchinson *Scottish Politics in the Twentieth Century*
Roger Mason *Kingship and Tyranny? Scotland 1513–1603*
John McCaffrey *Scotland in the Nineteenth Century*
John Shaw *The Political History of Eighteenth-Century Scotland*
Bruce Webster *Scotland in the Middle Ages*

History of Wales

Gareth Jones *Wales, 1700–1980: Crisis of Identity*

Please note that a sister series, *Social History in Perspective*, is now available. It covers the key topics in social, cultural and religious history.

THE BRITISH REPUBLIC
1649–1660

RONALD HUTTON

Lecturer in History
University of Bristol

MACMILLAN

First published 1990 by
THE MACMILLAN PRESS LTD
Houndmills, Basingstoke, Hampshire RG21 2XS
and London
Companies and representatives
throughout the world

ISBN 0–333–40463–7 hardcover
ISBN 0–333–40464–5 paperback

A catalogue record for this book is available
from the British Library.

12 11 10 9 8 7 6 5 4
03 02 01 00 99 98 97 96 95

Printed in Hong Kong

CONTENTS

For the Peerage of Redbridge,
long ago:
Bramwell Tovey,
David Pearl
and
Christopher Freeman

PREFACE

I agreed to write this book at the importunity of a friend, the commissioning editor, Jeremy Black. It was the first which I had ever attempted which synthesised the work of many colleagues with my own, so that for much of the time I was deploying the research of others. As such, I found the prospect of it rather forbidding: it was 'microwaved history', a heap of everything that seemed to be known upon the subject, heated through briefly with my own opinions and served up to the general reader. It is the hardest type of book with which to please professional colleagues, for what accords with their opinions will seem familiar and dull to them, and what does not will often seem irritating. My principal reason for agreeing to undertake it was that it represented an opportunity to provide students and the general public with the very latest picture of an important episode of history, in an accessible form and at an accessible price. In doing so, I was also closing a gap between the two periods in which most of my existing work has been concentrated, the 1640s and the years from 1658 to 1685, and so completing a sequence of four books. Some of the ground was covered in my previous publications upon the Restoration and upon Charles II, and I have had to consider all of it during the years in which I ran a Special Subject upon the British Republic at Bristol University. It is customary for academics who chair such courses to comment upon the amount that they have learned from their students. I endorse this whole-heartedly, but

I have gained a great deal from three of them in particular: Dominic Stuttaford, Bruce Yardley and Philip Norrey. The last became a research student at Bristol and produced a superb doctoral thesis upon the Restoration period before having to seek employment outside academe because of the current absence of opportunities within it. Wherever you are when this book is published, Phil, I hope that it gives you pleasure, for you could have written it better than I.

INTRODUCTION

In February 1649 the three traditional British kingdoms were each dominated by a very different regime. England was a republic, with a nominally presbyterian national Church and a *de facto* toleration of more radical Protestant religious groups. Scotland was a kingdom, with a presbyterian Kirk fiercely intolerant of any variety of dissent. Ireland was almost wholly controlled by monarchists who had agreed upon a religious settlement guaranteeing freedom of worship to Roman Catholics and episcopalian Protestants. Although only one of these regimes (the Irish confederacy) can definitely be said to have enjoyed the support of a majority of the population which it controlled, all were powerful enough to defeat any domestic enemies. Each was therefore independently viable: the problem was that none was prepared to recognise the existence of the others. This was resolved within three years, with the conquest of Scotland and Ireland by the English republicans, leading to the union of all three states in a Parliament sitting at Westminster. Within a decade more, this creation had in turn been transformed, into three independent monarchies, united in the person of a king seated at Westminster. The tale of the Interregnum in British history is therefore one of how a small group of English, in every sense unrepresentative of their nation, gained and lost control of the whole British archipelago. They therefore occupy the central position in this book, interacting with all the national, political, religious, social and linguistic groups of their islands.

Before considering their story, it may be worthwhile to emphasise how complex a matter it was, and how difficult it is to portray intelligibly the patterns of events. Let us glance briefly at the activities of a handful of people at the time of the great symbolic action which terminated the English monarchy, the execution of King Charles I. As the axe fell, a young gentleman called John Evelyn was living at his father-in-law's house in Deptford, Kent. Devoted by instinct to the monarchy, he was overcome with horror at the news and fasted through the whole fatal day. Yet Evelyn's reaction was not simply that of a loyal royalist. Sincere though his beliefs were, he had gone upon an educational tour of Europe during the Civil War rather than take the risk of fighting for them. His sorrow may have been intensified by guilt. Furthermore, he had been expecting that the King would come to terms with his enemies, and hoped for a job in the resulting administration which would help him to build up an estate. His career prospects had fallen with his sovereign's head and Evelyn had more to mourn than the monarchy. Forty miles to the north, at the village of Earl's Colne in Essex, the vicar, Ralph Josselin, was entering up his diary. Only a few years older than Evelyn, Josselin's views had been utterly different. He had hailed the defeat of the King's partisans with joy. Yet, upon hearing of the regicide, he found himself weeping. This was in part a fear that the sheer boldness of the act would risk the anger of God. With smallpox already in the village and all foodstuffs very expensive after the worst harvest for a generation, Earl's Colne needed no more manifestations of divine displeasure. But Josselin was also seriously upset by the divisions which the great event had opened among his parishioners. The more ignorant and irresponsible they were, the more passionately they expressed themselves upon the subject, and their quarrels troubled the minister so much that he could not keep up his Hebrew studies. Some of them may have resembled John Norris, a London tailor. He was either cautious or lucky for a year after the King's death, but on 27 April 1650, at the church of St Botolph's-without-Aldgate, he became neither. He allegedly launched into a diatribe against Charles I's executioners, and found himself indicted for it at Middlesex

Quarter Sessions. The evidence was good enough for the jury to send him for trial, but we do not know what happened thereafter. It is entirely possible that he had been denounced by private enemies and had never spoken the words at all, so we do not quite know what to make of his case. Over at Yeovil in Somerset economic, not political concerns had got Dorothy Beacham into court. Her husband had died in the Civil War, serving with Sir Arthur Hesilrige's regiment, leaving her with three children and dependent upon the charity of an impoverished community. At Easter 1649, having gone through the winter following that record harvest failure, she was desperate enough to petition the republic's first Quarter Sessions for relief. But here her luck came in, for the regicide had ensured the domination of the Somerset Bench by allies of Hesilrige. She got a lump sum and an order for a handsome pension: while not herself 'concerned' in national affairs, they had first wrecked and then partly repaired her life. In Warwickshire, during the same round of Quarter Sessions, another widow was also active. She was accusing a labourer from Priors Hardwick, called Thomas Richardson, of having taken one of her ewes. We do not know the result. The republic executed sheep-stealers exactly as the monarchy had done, and we must believe that Richardson had more pressing concerns upon his mind at this time than national affairs. But we cannot assume that he had no views upon them. As with so many people like him, who are mere names in county and parish records, his place in the political pattern may simply be lost.

This rapid series of portraits suffices to demonstrate the fundamental problem. The 'true' history of the British Republic could only be written if we understood the opinions and activities of every individual who resided in it. For the great majority we have no information, while for most of the remainder it is incomplete or untrustworthy. In the few cases where it is full, we find ironies and complications which might not have been expected on a first glance at the person concerned. We see the past in mirrors, which in turn capture only reflections made upon streams.

1

THE COMMONWEALTH

I The Central Regime

The King's execution, on 30 January 1649, was of course just the
great dramatic centrepiece to a series of constitutional developments. From 6 December the army nominally at the command of
the English Parliament had enforced the purging from the House
of Commons of two-thirds of its members.[1] It was the remnant
who set up Charles's trial, and went on in March to abolish the
monarchy and the House of Lords before constituting themselves the governing body of a 'Commonwealth and free state' of
England in May. These were the most drastic changes to have
occurred in the English state since its appearance, removing
two-thirds of the components of the national legislature and
altering the source of sovereignty for both the executive and the
judiciary. They thus amply deserve the name of the 'English
Revolution', in the sense that the landmarks of national politics
had been almost completely altered.

The toppled institutions had gone down like dominoes as the
army and its allies in the Commons struggled with the problem
of Charles I. Once they had decided that he was impossible to
deal with and had to be put on trial, they had to purge
Parliament down to those MPs willing to effect this, or to
dissolve the whole Parliament and give the job to an interim
government. Once the purge had occurred, and the King still
refused to accept their terms, he had to be killed. Since his heirs

4

were on the Continent, plotting revenge, the monarchy was abolished. The Lords went because none of them would support the regicide and the number who might have worked with the Commonwealth was too pitiful to make up a quorum. This was the logic of events, but it is important to bear in mind the sheer pitch of emotion with which the soldiers were acting. All through the previous summer they had been fighting for their lives and beliefs in the so-called Second Civil War against a great coalition constructed by the King. This included not only many of his traditional supporters from the Great Civil War which had ended in 1646, but many old opponents from that war who had turned against the victorious Parliament. By a mixture of good luck and brilliant fighting, Parliament's army had beaten the lot. Then it had turned with fury upon its tormentor, Charles Stuart, and in its efforts to get at him had wrecked the English constitution.

It is a reflection of the discrepancy in evidence, but also, per-haps, of distaste, that historians have tended to focus upon the civilian or parliamentary radicals of the age, rather than these soldiers, the men who made the English Revolution. For their time, they were an extraordinary group of people. One very unusual thing about them was that so many of their leaders were of relatively humble social origins. Of the total officer corps in 1648, half came from backgrounds so obscure that no informa-tion can be recovered about them. Of the remainder, nearly half came from the middle and lower ranks of society, especially from the towns. Only 9 per cent of the total had received any higher education, and a sixth of them had definitely been promoted from the ranks.[2] The highest levels of the corps contained more gentry, but also former artisans. This structure is important to remember, because in late 1648 it was the junior officers and the men who were making the political running. The Commander-in-Chief, Lord Fairfax, allowed himself to be bound by the deci-sions of his subordinates, and kept entirely aloof from the King's trial. The Lieutenant-General, Oliver Cromwell, was at first hesitant. He slowly came to endorse the cry of his men for justice upon Charles, arrived in London only after the Commons had been purged, and spent his first weeks there trying to promote a last-minute deal with the King. It was when Charles's obstinacy made regicide inevitable that Cromwell took control of the process and became the superintendent of the trial and execution. Of the army's nominal leaders it was the third in rank, the Commissary-General of the Horse, Henry Ireton, who sponsored the call to try Charles and the decision to purge the Commons. But in September he had gone on leave because of the lack of support which his proposals were receiving among the other general officers. He only returned triumphantly in November when a succession of regimental petitions to Fairfax made it clear that many junior officers and privates shared his views. Although the army was quartered across the country, its unanimity on the question of the King is striking. Units stationed in Yorkshire wanted him brought to justice just as strongly as those in the London area.

Thus it could be said that the Revolution was effected by people who came from outside the traditional political order and were therefore the more prepared to pull it down. But the crucial fact about this army is not that it was largely officered by commoners, but that they were commoners who had been through a very special experience. For one thing, they had opportunities to gain wealth and prestige denied to most from their backgrounds. The infantry, it is true, were paid slightly less than agricultural labourers, but the cavalry received more than twice as much and promotion to officer status meant a very handsome salary. Furthermore, it was an army which operated very much by mutual consultation. Before every important military action the generals would confer with all colonels present and some inferior officers, allowing free debate to all. In 1647, after the end of the Great Civil War, Parliament had tried to disband much of the army and to send the rest to Ireland, without ensuring good terms for either demobilisation or service. The soldiers had mutinied, appointing representatives from each regiment to confer with the officers in a General Council, and forced Parliament to accept most of their demands. In religion also, the army operated in a manner quite unlike that of the bulk of the population. Partly because of a number of radical chaplains, and partly because of a lack of chaplains at all, many soldiers had become accustomed to hold prayer-meetings of their own and to listen to sermons from certain officers. By 1648 it is possible that the majority of them were worshipping in congregations gathered around pastors chosen by themselves without any reference to the national Church. This was an arrangement probably shared by, at most, 1 per cent of the civilian population. Finally, the experience of war was itself very important. During the summer of 1648, as said, the soldiers had undergone once more all the terror, exhilaration, sorrow and triumph of active service. Their sense of the implications of politics and their sense of divine providence would both have been heightened in a way not accessible to many other people.

There were several reasons why this army should have been feeling angry in the autumn of 1648. One was that its rates of pay had not been raised since it was formed, while after the recent bad harvests the price of food had greatly risen (that of bread more than doubled). Another was that even this relatively diminishing amount of money was not being delivered. The disruption caused by the summer's fighting had told upon the fiscal machinery and also provided opportunities for tax evasion by a population tired of burdens and often hostile to the soldiers' cause. As a result, many regiments were paying for their food, drink and lodging with tickets which were to be redeemed if money came in. Throughout the autumn Parliament did nothing to remedy this situation. Instead, it seemed determined to ignore and to slight the army. It declared that officers who came to London to enquire about their arrears would lose their right to the whole amount. It kept bargaining with a King who had just fomented a new Civil War in which many of its soldiers had died. In August it passed an ordinance for a presbyterian Church of England without toleration of independent congregations of the sort so common amongst the army. On 2 December it decided to effect a militia system which might render the army itself redundant. Most observers recognised that the bulk of both Lords and Commons regarded the soldiers as a temporary unpleasant necessity, disliked both as a potential political threat and as a hotbed of religious radicalism. Charles I had fought the Great Civil War to avoid having to surrender his control over

Why kill [handwritten margin note]

ministerial appointments and the armed forces, and to accept the removal of bishops from the Church. Having lost that war and become Parliament's prisoner he had still refused those terms, devoting his energies instead to dividing his former enemies and to preparing for another armed struggle. Having lost that struggle in turn, during 1648, he would not concede the same demands even now, save as an interim settlement, and was trying to obtain military aid from Ireland and France. When the Commons voted on 5 December to accept his replies as a basis for negotiation, this seemed to the army to represent the final proof that the MPs were going to sell out to Charles in order to provide the swiftest opportunity to get rid of their soldiers. The next morning a detachment of these soldiers, commanded by Colonel Pride, was at the door of the Commons to carry out the purge, and showed their hatred and contempt for the members whom they excluded.

In many ways, then, the army was acting defensively. But it did have a positive programme to offer as well, remarkable both in its audacity and in the consistency with which it had been pursued over time. In 1647, when the soldiers were defying Parliament over the questions of disbanding and service in Ireland, they had presented their own terms to Charles, the so-called *Heads of Proposals*. Agreed upon by the officers (Ireton again being prominent) and their allies in the Lords and Commons, they represented a sharp contrast to those being offered to the King by the majority in Parliament. Whereas the latter had been concerned with redistributing power within an existing system, the *Heads* aimed to change the system itself. They allowed Charles to regain control of the armed forces more swiftly than Parliament had been prepared to do, and were also more generous in permitting him some voice in the choice of ministers. They were also more lenient towards the defeated royalists and made possible the retention of a weak episcopacy. But all this was made conditional upon the toleration of independent religious congregations, plus the creation of a powerful Council to advise the monarch, and a series of parliaments, elected by a uniform franchise and from seats redistributed to reflect recent changes in wealth and population. This initiative failed because Charles deflected it along with all other terms *Reys* offered to him. During the autumn of 1647 some regiments demanded more extensive reforms, including the abolition of the remaining royal powers, a codification of the law and a more extensive parliamentary franchise. Cromwell and Ireton met a Council of Officers and some representatives from other ranks at Putney to debate against these propositions but further discussion was aborted by the growing military crisis created by Charles's machinations. In November 1648, when the regimental petitions for the King's trial flowed in to Fairfax, he called a Council of the officers quartered in the London area. This eventually agreed to offer Charles the *Heads of Proposals* with some further restrictions upon his authority, but even before his refusal was received the gathering had turned to an alternative policy suggested by Ireton. This was to address Parliament, for their arrears of pay, for the trial of the King, the outlawing of his heirs and the punishment of his principal followers, and for the electoral reforms outlined in the *Heads*. As thrashed out by the officers, the plan allowed for an elected monarch without a veto over legislation. When the Houses received this package on 20 November, they first shelved and then rejected it. On the 29th the Council of Officers resolved to march into London, to dissolve Parliament and then to call its allies in the Commons to form a caretaker government until a Parliament could meet under the reformed system. What altered this plan into a purge was the insistence of the MPs prepared to work with the army, that dissolution would be a slower and less effective way of dealing with immediate problems such as that of the King.

As the Purged Parliament set about Charles's trial, the Council of Officers, now numbering 73, was debating the form of the Commonwealth. Ireton usually presided over these discussions and, as at Putney, the junior officers present tended to want more fundamental reforms. Because of the democratic practices of the gathering, the colonels were repeatedly voted down by their subordinates. As a result, it was agreed to forbid conscription, to prevent any Parliament from wielding emergency powers outside the law of the land, and to deprive magistrates of power to regulate the religious activities of radical

9

B ground

Protestants. The final document provided for the dissolution of the Purged Parliament by May, and the election of a new one according to the reforms proposed in the *Heads*. There was to be a national Church, but attendance of it was to be voluntary and so would be the payment of tithes, the hitherto compulsory rate levied upon all parishioners for the upkeep of the minister. Worship outside it was permitted to all except Roman Catholics and those who used the pre-war Prayer Book which had become associated with the royalist party. The whole plan was called *The Agreement of the People*.

Thus far the story resembles that of many later revolutions. A cadre of radicals had seized power by armed force, equipped with a blueprint for a new political system. If there was a dominant figure amongst them, it seemed to be Ireton, who was himself virtually the type of the later romantic revolutionary leader: relatively young (not yet forty), brooding, reserved, incorruptible, tireless in the pursuit of his ideals. But he was not to be the presiding genius of the Commonwealth, and the army's programme was not to be enacted either rapidly or completely. At its basis lay an enduring weakness: that the soldiers were only prepared to rule through civilians, and that they had almost no civilian friends.

This may be illustrated by looking at those groups who ought to have been, and at times were, the army's allies. During the 1640s the crucial issue which had divided the victorious parliamentarian party of the Great Civil War was that of the existence of Protestant congregations independent of the established Church of England. Virtually all agreed upon the proscription of Catholic worship and the use of the old Prayer Book, but most wanted to replace both with a presbyterian Church and to enforce conformity to it, and it was this policy which parliament had pursued until Pride's Purge. During the war years, between the collapse of the old episcopal Church and the establishment of the new system, a number of independent congregations had been formed. The majority, numbering thirty-six, were in London, but they also existed in provincial towns and (as has been stressed) in the army. Indeed, the latter regularly planted such churches in the garrison towns, while some former soldiers founded them upon returning to civilian life. Since the end of the Great Civil War they had continued to survive because the continuing political turmoil prevented the establishment of the projected intolerant presbyterianism. Pride's Purge removed almost all the proponents of the latter from parliament. Thus the creation of the Commonwealth was more or less synonymous with legal toleration of such congregations and those who believed in such a thing were its 'natural' supporters.

This said, they represented two problems for Ireton and his military colleagues. One has already been stated: that they formed a tiny percentage of the English and Welsh in general. The other was, of course, that they could disagree amongst themselves upon an immense range of issues. In religious matters alone, they differed over the importance of the Scriptures, sacred buildings, rituals and a priestly or ministerial order, the choice between adult or infant baptism, theories of salvation, restrictions upon membership and the problem of whether to retain the national Church. One thing that all of them had in common was a heightened sense of the importance of religion, so that such bickering was inevitable. But for political purposes there were two divisions which surpassed all others in significance. One was between those who believed that a pastor ought to mediate between God and a body of worshippers, and those who believed that every person with sufficient faith could unite with God personally. The second was between those who felt that most humans were irredeemably corrupt and that the godly would always be an embattled minority, and those who believed that almost anybody could be saved, given the right teaching. If somebody tended to the second of each of those choices, then a religious, political and social radicalism was possible to them which could arouse stark horror even among many who believed in toleration of different Protestant groups. By 1646 contemporaries were trying to classify the various types of religious belief being propounded in England, in terms of sects or 'heresies'. It is perhaps better to think of a relatively small number of very active individuals, many of them altering their ideas and associates over time.

Nevertheless, as soon as they intervened in national politics in 1647, army officers had to reckon with a particular interest group among the more extreme political and religious thinkers of the metropolis. Historians have called them the 'Levellers', which, like so many political labels originated as a term of abuse by opponents, has stuck for lack of a suitable alternative. At times modern writers have spoken of them as if they were a mass movement, at others as if they consisted of three intellectuals equipped with a printing press. Some writers have portrayed them as an external force to the army, acting upon it, others as a group which spanned soldiers and civilians. In some respects all these viewpoints are true. The three intellectuals concerned were William Walwyn, Richard Overton and John Lilburne. Walwyn was the presiding personality of the trio, Lilburne the most flamboyant and energetic, but all were brilliant pamphleteers. They had come together in London in 1645, to appeal to Parliament for freedom of religious beliefs. As the months passed, their programme expanded to include safeguards against arbitrary arrest, the use of English (not Latin) in law courts, an extension of the franchise, the abolition of trade monopolies and the end of press censorship. Their political attitudes altered, as those of the army were to do, in response to the opposition which they encountered. In 1646 the House of Lords arrested Lilburne, whereupon the three of them henceforth denied the peers a major role in government, and directed their campaign wholly at the Commons. By 1647, realising that the Lower House was proving almost equally unresponsive, they were ready to turn to the army as it defied Parliament and formulated its own terms to the King.

These three men were the most celebrated and visible of those who became dubbed Levellers, but they had many allies and supporters. Some came from those independent congregations which believed in universal salvation, while others, such as their fellow-Londoner John Wildman, seemed to belong to no church. Their power-base lay in the capital, with some associated groups in its environs and in a zone stretching westward across Buckinghamshire and Oxfordshire to Bristol and Worcester. They could raise scores of thousands of signatures for petitions, yet these represented no more than a significant minority of a metropolitan population of almost half a million. The leaders, like the army officers, came from a mixed social background, younger children of gentry working with people from mercantile, artisan or quite obscure backgrounds. Their policies were aimed principally at small traders and manufacturers, but Lilburne himself did not seem to be quite sure who followed him in practice. Sometimes he spoke of 'the middling sort' and sometimes of 'leather aprons'. Equally vexed is the question of their influence in the army. In mid-1646 shocked presbyterians were noting that some soldiers already believed in general religious toleration and the reform of the legal system and franchise, without knowing whether they had been swayed by civilian writers. It can only be stated certainly that in 1647 the London radicals and those within the army encouraged each other in demanding more extensive changes than those envisaged in the *Heads of Proposals*. By September they were working closely together and Wildman, though a civilian, attended the debates at Putney. In the autumn of 1648 similar collaboration took place. The regimental petitions for the King's trial were shortly preceded, and perhaps precipitated, by one from the Levellers. On 28 November Lilburne appeared at Ireton's quarters and persuaded him to let the new constitution be drafted by a mixture of army officers, his own associates, MPs and ministers of the London gathered churches. It was this draft which was laid before the Council of Officers in December and amended by them, although their debates were attended by some of Lilburne's civilian friends and some of the ministers as well. Thus the *Agreement of the People* was a co-operative effort of military and civilian thinkers, the former determining the eventual result.

Unhappily for all concerned, the co-operation was somewhat illusory. For one thing, the thought of Lilburne and his comrades had been evolving in the course of 1648, in ways that made it even less compatible with that of men like Ireton. Although they disagreed among themselves over details, they had become wedded to the idea that true civil liberty involved an enormous decentralisation of government and the revitalisation of the small community. They wanted local law courts, local election of officials and local systems of defence. They expected an end to heavy central taxation. Such a utopia had no place for an army of the sort that Ireton and his colleagues commanded. Further-more, Lilburne himself had already washed his hands of the *Agreement* because the original draft had been altered by the military. He and his associates were people who would test any form of government against an ideal and attack it vehemently if they found it wanting. Their attitude was one which leads, almost inevitably, to martyrdom.

The likely fate of the *Agreement* was not made happier by the complexion of the Purged Parliament, to whom the officers delivered it, for further consideration, on 20 January. After Pride's Purge many of the MPs who had not been excluded still withdrew from the House to return only when the regicide was accomplished. The presiding body of the new Commonwealth was therefore composed in large part (almost half) of people who had grave reservations about the events which had brought that Commonwealth into existence. As a body, it was socially far more prestigious than the army officers. True, those MPs who had attended the House all the way though the King's trial tended to come from families slightly less well-established than those who had been purged, and fewer of them had received higher education. But the main non-ideological distinction be-tween the two was that the 'revolutionary' MPs were often in financial trouble and had lent a lot of money to the parliamen-tary cause which they needed to have repaid. Over half of the purged House were still people who, in pre-Civil War days, would have been among the rulers of their native counties. In turn, they looked for leadership to those amongst them who enjoyed the greatest possible social rank. Their views were also rather different from those of the army. Only a few of the latter's officers sat in the House themselves, of whom the most dedicated to reform was Ireton himself, who still found some of the *Agreement* too radical for his tastes. Only four other MPs, out of a total of 213 now allowed to sit, had ever shown enthusiasm for changes of the extent proposed in that document. Those who had actively supported the regicide were more interested in persuading their more cautious colleagues to support the

Commonwealth than in enacting further reforms. In February the House appointed some of its supposedly most radical members to propose names for the Council of State which was to operate as its executive body. Barely half of those whom they recommended had sat in either the Parliament, or the tribunal which had condemned the King, during the past month. The list was adopted, and with a further snub to the army. First, the MPs debated whether its officers should be allowed to be on the Council at all, and then they barred from it Ireton and another colonel who had been actively concerned in the march upon London to purge the Commons. As a result the only serving officers included were Fairfax, who had refused to attend the King's trial, and Cromwell, who had secured his credit with the soldiers by promoting it but now won regard in the House by encouraging doubtful MPs to resume their seats. This, of course, further limited its potential to be a reforming body. When Ireton tried at least to have all the new councillors express approval of the regicide, Cromwell won acceptance instead for an undertaking that they would accept the Commonwealth for the future.

To be fair to the new government, it was in a position of appalling insecurity and suffering considerable distractions. Scotland was passively, and most of Ireland actively, hostile. The royalists still had privateer bases in the Scilly Isles, Jersey and the Isle of Man, and a powerful fleet operating out of Irish ports. Not a single foreign state came forward to recognise the Commonwealth, and most were shocked by the unprecedented act of the King's execution. His heir, now styling himself Charles II, was the guest of the Dutch, who maintained one of the world's most formidable navies. At home the Revolution threatened to halt all the normal processes of civil government unless they could be swiftly recast in a republican form. Accordingly, during the first three months after the regicide, the Purged Parliament set frantically about two different tasks. One was to build up the English navy, by ordering the construction of 77 warships of the latest design and conscripting thousands of seamen (in defiance of *The Agreement of the People*). The other task was to commission panels of MPs to carry out key tasks such as running the Admiralty and using a newly-made republican

Great Seal to validate official documents. Over half the existing judges refused to accept the Commonwealth, and the rest (who included the Speaker of the Purged Parliament) only agreed to do so upon assurances that it would uphold the 'fundamental laws of the land'. The latter were not defined, but the promise was generally taken to be a pledge against radical reform. The judicial bench was filled up with respected lawyers from important gentry families, stressing again that the new regime was bidding for widespread acceptance.

However, one action of the new Commonwealth was guaranteed to offend radicals and conservatives alike. One of the things demanded by the army at the time of Pride's Purge had been vengeance upon the leaders of the royalist risings of 1648 as well as upon the King. While the Purged Parliament viewed reform with distaste, it was happy to throw the soldiers some sacrificial victims. In the political circumstances it was likely that a jury chosen by normal practice would acquit the accused. So the Parliament decided to proceed, as against the King, by impanelling tribunals which would act as both judges and jurors. The device was effective, and three royalist nobles were beheaded. But it was a flagrant violation of every declaration of civil rights since Magna Carta, and for Walwyn, Overton and Lilburne it was too much. They issued pamphlets denouncing the new regime as hypocritical, corrupt and despotic, and were committed to the Tower in March. Their arrest split the radical groups of the City. Those gathered churches who believed that only a handful of saints could escape damnation had looked with increasing disfavour upon the Levellers' plans to disperse power to the masses. In December the Purged Parliament had imposed new qualifications for the election of London's Common Council. As a result, half of the corporation was replaced, giving power over the City to those who would support the Commonwealth. At least for the time being, some radicals were satisfied with that. Many of the independent congregations accordingly addressed the Purged Parliament to disassociate themselves from Lilburne and his friends. On the other hand, support for the Levellers would now be expanded by people who disliked the Commonwealth for any reason. And there was the crucial question of the army.

The soldiers had almost as much reason for grievance in early 1649 as in late 1648. Apart from insulting them while setting up the Council of State, and utterly ignoring the *Agreement of the People*, the Purged Parliament had done nothing about their pay. In March the Council of Officers petitioned it about the matter. They did at least receive a courteous reply, and the obvious need to attend to the navy did excuse some of the MPs' behaviour. The problem had itself been eased very slightly. During the winter, while Ireton was attending to the *Agreement* and Cromwell to the regicide, Fairfax was preoccupied with the issue of money for his men. The new corporation of London worked with him to get the City's taxes paid in full, and he sponsored a system whereby the money paid by specific counties went to specific regiments, facilitating its allocation. But there was still a large shortfall, and in April some troopers in London refused to remove to quarters in Essex unless they got some cash. They had to be rounded up by force, and their leader shot. By now the Purged Parliament was working on the matter, raising the level of the land tax or 'assessment' (the principal source of revenue) by a third, abolishing the Deans and Chapters of the Church of England, and offering their lands for sale to raise more funds. It was almost too late. As in 1647, it was the issue of service in Ireland which pushed a discontented army into defiance. In April units for an expeditionary force to that land were chosen by lot at Fairfax's headquarters, without any reference to the views of their members. In early May two horse regiments quartered in Wiltshire mutinied, objecting to this treatment, to the terms which they were being given for the service and to their present lack of pay. They demanded a General Council for the army, with all ranks represented. At once Fairfax and Cromwell formed a crack force and marched upon them. The mutineers rode north, trying to join other discontented units in the Midlands, but were forced to the west by their pursuers and surprised by them while resting at Burford on the 14th. Three of their leaders were executed in the churchyard. In the 1980s it became a custom for radical socialists to go upon pilgrimage to Burford to honour these dead, according to an historical orthodoxy that the dissident soldiers had risen to achieve the

Levellers' dream. Certainly the Levellers had been trying their utmost to suborn the army, and hailed the mutineers (as they had done those in London in April) as comrades. Conversely, Fairfax and Cromwell accused them of Leveller sympathies to help justify their punishment. Agitators formerly associated with Lilburne and Wildman were prominent among the malcontent soldiery. But it is worth stressing that the mutineers themselves, both in April and May, only objected to conditions of service.[3] The modern pilgrims who gather at Burford should only be there if they care passionately about the pay of the armed forces. On the other hand, a genuine Leveller rising did take place simultaneously in Oxfordshire, of militiamen and armed citizens inspired by William Thompson, a former soldier who had been cashiered in 1647 after being convicted of a violent crime. As the dissident regiments were broken at Burford, so was Thompson's band, near Wellingborough. He fought to the death alone in a wood. The latter would indeed be an appropriate place for pilgrimage by modern radicals, but alas! No account of his last stand fixes its location.

In the course of these dramatic events, the date fixed in the *Agreement of the People* for the dissolution of the Purged Parliament slipped past, ignored by its members. Instead, as the mutineers rode towards Burford, the MPs at last raised the soldiers' rates of pay generously, to take account of inflation. In June they decided to sell off the Crown lands, which had since the foundation of the English state been one of its great capital assets, and to employ the proceeds to satisfy the army's arrears. From the summer onwards, for over two years, much of the army was engaged in fighting in various parts of the British Isles, and so less active in central politics. During the same summer the Council of State released Walwyn and Overton, and allowed Lilburne trial by a jury, which acquitted him. But without the prospect of help from the soldiery, those Levellers still active were helpless. The Purged Parliament thus had a breathing space in which to settle the nation.

What it did was to provide for the war effort, very efficiently, and to tinker with every other problem. Its behaviour was enforced by the fact that it was pulled powerfully in two opposed ideological directions at once. One was the course suggested by the instinct of the majority of its own members: to consolidate what had already been achieved and to persuade the nation, and especially its 'natural' ruling class, to accept it. The other was that urged by the army, which was still determined that further reform should occur. The combined effect of good pay and active service had only been that the soldiers were prepared to allow more time for this. The resulting conflict is seen most obviously in the great matter of religion. The *Agreement of the People* had, as said, prescribed a national Church, with toleration of Protestant dissenters but without the compulsory payment of tithes. Most of the MPs wanted a presbyterian system, with a carefully circumscribed toleration of dissent and with tithes levied upon everybody. Some members of the army, and some gathered congregations, were meanwhile becoming convinced of the need to abolish the Church of England and the whole clerical profession, together with the universities. These were reforms more radical than any that the Levellers had called for, and advocated by preachers with fundamentally different instincts. Whereas Lilburne and his allies had wanted to decentralise power to the masses, the new men believed in concentrating it in the hands of a few, who would carry out the changes over the heads of the 'ungodly' majority. The most millenarian of them were becoming known as 'Fifth Monarchy Men', after the rule of the saints promised in the Book of Daniel. In fear of them, a group of ministers of independent churches came to believe in the need both for a national Church, loosely organised, and a national creed. These were led by John Owen, whom the Purged Parliament made Dean of Christ Church, Oxford, and they began co-operating with moderate presbyterians. The religious pressure-groups of the nation were thus altering in nature and growing in complexity.

In late 1649 the Purged Parliament tried to establish presbyterianism as the national religion but, in the face of a hostile petition from the army, the courage of the MPs receded and they scrapped the plan by one vote. Instead, in this year and the next, they enacted measures likely to appeal to a wide range of opinion. They allocated revenues taken from the Crown, bishops, deans and chapters to augment the stipends of poor ministers. They vested others in commissions of supporters of the Commonwealth in the four northernmost counties and in Wales, intended to improve the provision of Church services in those areas. This was done in response to petitions from those supporters, but the commissioners proceeded to offend presbyterian opinion by appointing itinerant preachers, sometimes of notably radical views. The Parliament, accordingly, allowed both experiments to lapse. As the church courts which had punished moral offences had vanished with the bishops and deans, adultery, incest and fornication were made secular crimes. The penalty for all was stiffened, in the first two cases to death, a development with which many presbyterians would agree. Likewise the punishment for swearing was made harsher, and certain extreme religious opinions (such as declaring oneself to be Christ, or claiming that saints were free from all moral constraints) were called blasphemy and made illegal. Only in late 1650, responding to a new radical initiative among its members and from the army, did the Parliament repeal the laws enjoining attendance of the national Church, provided that all people were present at some service. This granted the minimum demand of the independent congregations, but left the nature of the Church itself undecided. The Purged Parliament debated it, and the problem of a substitute for tithes, for the remainder of its existence. In February 1652 John Owen's group of ministers presented a plan for the regulation of the national clergy and for a definition of acceptable doctrine. The congregations which rejected the concept of an established Church, and a set of army officers led by Pride, mounted a campaign against these proposals, and soon these too got bogged down in discussions.

Even less progress was made in legal reform. It had been obvious for decades that the great central courts, especially that of Chancery, were overworked and thus slow and expensive to use. Many people recognised a need to reconstruct them. On the other hand, the Fifth Monarchists and some other radicals wanted to abolish the whole legal profession and to abbreviate the law to a simple code. The Purged Parliament, again, enacted a set of minor changes while discussing major reforms. It relieved poor debtors and abolished some writs and fees, the use of Latin and stylised handwriting in court records, and the legal privileges of peers and MPs. It empowered the common law courts to grant probate of wills, which had been a function of the vanished Church tribunals. But all the fundamental problems of the system remained. A similar record of prolonged hesitation characterised the Parliament's attempts to settle the future government of the country. The army had created it to be an interim regime, and the longer that it sat, the more it would appear to the nation at large to be nothing more than a self-seeking oligarchy. The draft *Agreement of the People*, in December 1648, had mandated it to dissolve as soon as it had provided for an electoral system of 300 seats, all distributed on the basis of population. Of these seats 14 per cent would represent boroughs, and the rest counties, reversing the traditional system whereby the great majority represented boroughs, which were commonly more vulnerable to manipulation by patrons. As amended by the officers, the *Agreement* provided for 400 seats, distributed on a basis of local wealth, and gave 20 per cent of these to boroughs. Both schemes had excluded royalists from the franchise, at least for a time, and envisaged the election of a Parliament every two years. The numbing worry which beset the purged House, and which does not seem to have occurred to many in the army, was that a large number of the potential electorate who had never been royalists were opposed to the Commonwealth and all that it stood for. There was a real probability that the complexion of the next Parliament would be that of the existing one before it was purged. Accordingly, the MPs approved the officers' scheme in principle but failed to enact it.

Given this situation, it is not surprising that the Commonwealth was somewhat insecure in its identity and that this reflected upon its ideology and its propaganda. The removal of Charles I had essentially been an act of tyrannicide, the destruction of a bad king, for which there were many historical precedents and arguments. But no people before had formally tried and executed their monarch for crimes against themselves, and there was absolutely no tradition of republican thought in England. Some English intellectuals had admired the supposed

21

virtues of the Roman Republic, and during the life of the Purged Parliament a group of its members and supporters, surrounding Henry Neville, Algernon Sidney and Thomas Chaloner, drew flattering parallels between Rome and the new republic. But their ideas were very much those of a small and erudite clique, and even in their case the task was one of trying to justify an event produced by emotion and expediency rather than by theory. In defending itself to the world and to its subjects, the strongest argument of the Commonwealth lay in its sheer military success. The editor of its principal newspaper, Marchamont Nedham, employed ancient history lavishly to set the English Republic in a glorious tradition, but much more important than these exhortations, to most people, were the unending series of victories which he could report. This record made a simple justification of the regime possible, and it was deployed principally by the pamphleteers Francis Rous and Anthony Ascham. They argued that as divine providence seemed to favour the Commonwealth, it was both pious and sensible to obey it. The Purged Parliament made its own actions suit this argument. It continued to execute people who fought or conspired against it, heading the list with another royalist earl and a distinguished London presbyterian. For their trials it reverted to the practice of empowering tribunals without juries, and when Lilburne continued to denounce the government, it sent him into exile abroad. In 1650 the Parliament imposed a declaration of loyalty upon all ministers of the Church and all office-holders, but (like that required of the Council of State) this only asked for a pledge of future support, not for approval of the regicide.

Such pragmatism had obvious moral weaknesses. The main one was pointed out by Edward Gee, who reminded Rous and Ascham that their argument made any political violence acceptable and destroyed any notion of the rule of law. It was also noteworthy that in none of its declarations did the new government attempt to defend itself by promising future reforms to benefit the nation. Indeed, it is probable that some of the Commonwealth's leaders toyed with the idea of establishing a form of monarchy. Unfortunately, the main source hitherto used to support this notion is unreliable. This is the retrospective account written by Bulstrode Whitelocke, one of the judges and Commissioners of the Great Seal. On 10 December 1651, according to Whitelocke, Cromwell called a meeting of army officers and MPs to discuss the future of the nation. Most of the lawyers and MPs there (led by Whitelocke himself) proposed the restoration of one of Charles I's sons as King. Most of the officers opposed this, and it was dropped. Cromwell himself, the passage notes, seemed to like the idea of monarchy, but not that of a Stuart at its head. Under the date 7 November 1652 Whitelocke reported a conversation with Cromwell, in which the latter proposed that he himself be made King. The judge replied that it would be better to restore Charles II. These entries have been quoted verbatim by several historians as if they were plain fact. Unfortunately, they were only written up a decade later, after the restoration of Charles had actually occurred and Whitelocke, as a former leader of the Commonwealth, was in danger of arrest. He would have had the strongest possible motive for portraying himself as a covert royalist, attempting to thwart the schemes of the general, who had in the intervening years come to be described by his enemies as a self-seeking schemer.

Certainly the prominence given to Cromwell in these passages does reflect his importance at the time when these events were set. In 1650 Fairfax had resigned the supreme command of the army rather than lead it against the Scots. He had never reconciled himself to the abolition of the monarchy and could not bring himself to invade the last monarchical state in the British Isles. In 1651 Ireton died in Ireland, having overworked himself until he collapsed. During the same period it was Cromwell who won the major victories in all theatres of war, and he was naturally appointed Lord General in succession to Fairfax. Once the wars were over, he threw himself into the work of mediating between the army and Parliament. While discountenancing the most radical propositions, such as the abolition of lawyers and clergy, he was always ready to speak for reform in general terms. Each time that soldiers expressed alarm at an initiative in the House, such as the move to establish presbyterianism or the plan presented by Owen's group, he urged the MPs to caution. The sheer dynamism of his personality made his role possible, for at one moment he could reassure presbyterians by speaking like a conservative country gentleman, at another confirm the confidence of his soldiers by using the language of a godly reformer. Far from guiding the Purged Parliament, however, his performance increased its ideological confusions and political paralysis.

By 1652 matters were starting to approach a crisis. Some of the Fifth Monarchists were now calling openly for the explusion of the MPs. Cromwell urged the army to patience and goodwill, but was careful to let its officers meet and express opinions, and these were increasingly hostile to the Parliament. Tension was increased by the fact that, if the Purged Parliament now included a dominant personality, it was that of Sir Arthur Hesilrige. Sir Arthur had much in common with Lilburne, in nature if not in beliefs. They had the same hasty temper, extrovert personality, unbudgeable attachment to their respective principles and fine eloquence, deployed without much reference to political realities. Hesilrige also spoke passionately for his country's liberties, but he could apparently only conceive of them as being served by himself and his colleagues in the purged House. In particular, he bitterly resented attempts by the army to put pressure upon them. Nonetheless, during the winter of 1652–3 confrontation was postponed by the apparent readiness of the Parliament to dissolve itself. Its work on the bill to qualify the future MPs, however, was so slow that by April the officers were very restless and Cromwell was having great difficulty in restraining them from expelling the MPs. He repeatedly urged the latter to make haste and then, on the 20th, he suddenly lost patience. In a towering rage he called in soldiers to clear the House, and so dissolved it. Why he made this decision must remain a mystery. He himself removed the crucial piece of evidence, the bill for the new elections which the MPs had been debating.[4] He then claimed that the Parliament had been attempting merely to recruit new members, not to dissolve, which seems to have been an outright lie. Something about the actions of the MPs had annoyed him, but we shall never know what it was. The upshot, however, was very clear: the army had created the Purged Parliament and then destroyed it for not having served its purpose. The only surprise was that the process had taken so long.

II The Localities

The previous chapter was concerned wholly with the problems of those in charge of England and Wales. The time has come to consider some of those experienced by the 5 million people whom they ruled. What did they think of the events of 1649–53? And how were they affected by them?

To begin to answer these questions it is necessary to understand the way in which most provincial commoners had regarded the political and social system before the Civil War. The essential fact was that they had thought it to be a relatively good system. Unlike the other states of its age, the English monarchy had combined a respected national representative body (Parliament) with a structure of taxation whereby the rich (in theory) paid most, an elaborate machinery of poor relief, and the jury system for trials. The national Church had enjoyed the loyalty of the overwhelming majority of people, who thought it to be the best in the world. Thus, even after the Great Civil War had shattered Church and State together and opened some minds to new possibilities, the instincts of the most radical reformers tended towards improving rather than demolishing the political and social structure. Even those who wanted to remove the Church or decentralise power had no plans to alter the institutions of local government (which represented government in general to most individuals), let alone to redistribute wealth within society. Furthermore, rural commoners in particular were principally concerned with issues such as grain shortages, the use of common land and the encroachment of drainage or disafforestation projects upon traditional rights. The Great Civil War had afforded them a tremendous opportunity to settle their grievances by taking the law into their own hands when public order broke down. At many places scattered up and down the country the property of unpopular landowners was attacked, drainage dykes breached and new enclosures levelled. As a result, by 1649 there were not many communities left which harboured acute resentment of their social superiors. The Levellers and the Fifth Monarchists both displayed little understanding of the world of the countryside. And within a few months of its accession to power, the Purged Parliament obliged a group of nobles and gentry by empowering them to drain a huge tract of fenland, in flagrant disregard of the wishes of the inhabitants.

There were good reasons why the Commonwealth should not have been popular with the English and Welsh in general. It had raised taxation to record levels and maintained an army which was quartered in the homes of many civilians. Historians can do no more than guess at the political views of the mass of the population, but every piece of evidence points to the conclusion that most people bitterly regretted the passing of the monarchy. Some indication of this is provided by the runaway success of *Eikon Basilike*, a volume put out just after the regicide which purported to contain the prayers and meditations of the dead King. It was utterly dishonest compilation, either heavily reworked or actually written by an opportunist clergyman, John Gauden, and perverting the truth of the past to foster the image of Charles I as saint and martyr. But its mawkish piety caught the public imagination so well that it went into a record thirty-five editions in English (and twenty-five in foreign tongues) in one year. When the Council of State asked John Milton to refute it, he commenced his reply with a recognition that the 'vulgar audience' responded easily to the book's sentiments. His own magnificent prose clearly did not, for his rebuttal of *Eikon* never made it to a second edition. Such tests of public political opinion are, however, rare and the historian's task is not much easier when examining attitudes to the Church under the Commonwealth.

One of the avowed aims of the Civil War parliamentarians had been to improve the quality of national religious life, by which they generally meant a more conscientious clergy with a better ability to preach. A negative tactic which they employed to secure this was to eject all clergy whom they considered to be unsatisfactory, among whom they naturally included royalists and confirmed neutralists who were otherwise excellent ministers. This process was continued under the Commonwealth, with the removal of clergy who preached against the new regime or refused the Engagement to be loyal to it. In Wales the commissioners 'for the Propagation of the Gospel', set up by the Purged Parliament, deprived 278 churchmen during the three years of their existence. It was quite impossible for them to find replacements for losses upon this scale, and they resorted to paying preachers stipends to travel around circuits. We do not know how well this device functioned, or how much satisfaction it gave parishioners. All that is certain is that, as recounted earlier, it frightened local gentry, and through them the Parliament, sufficiently to bring about the end of the scheme. In total, almost a fifth of the parish clergy of England were permanently deprived of their livings during the Civil War and under the republic. In some counties over a third went, while in Wales a shire such as Anglesey was practically denuded of its familiar ministers. This process would have pleased those parishes where the incumbent had been generally unpopular, but divided or caused widespread distress in others. The county committees of Parliament which performed the work relied upon information from local people, but too often this was provided by groups within a parish or its own partisans, who were not representative of majority opinion. Many ejected clergymen were reappointed at a later date, but never to their old benefices. Some ministers were paid extra to officiate temporarily in vacant livings, but this proved inadequate to the problem of supplying the places of those who had been evicted. In September 1648 forty parishes were vacant in London, Essex and Hertfordshire. The villagers of Toft, Cambridgeshire, had to wait six years before getting a new incumbent, and it must be presumed that such cases were as or more common in areas further from the capital. The parliamentarians had, however, a more positive programme as well: to augment the poorest livings with money taken from former Church revenues and from those of royalists. This work, also, was continued after Pride's Purge, but from start to finish the funds available for it were never sufficient. Thus, in Derbyshire 77 livings were augmented between 1645 and 1653, yet the number which afforded at least the minimum subsistence deemed adequate by the Parliament of 1624, was only raised to 62 per cent of the whole. And in some cases money was not forthcoming to provide even the increases which had been ordered.

The Commonwealth's failure either to impose a framework and a doctrine upon the Church of England or to dismantle it, naturally left all parties dissatisfied, but then it made none desperate. The result was a range of parochial practice determined, in different places, by the gentry, the minister or the parishioners. In some churches the pre-war Prayer Book was certainly read (illegally,) though the clergy involved sometimes only used extracts. Others employed the *Directory of Worship* made mandatory by Parliament in 1645, to replace the Prayer Book.[5] In London and Lancashire some parish clergy tried to restrict communion to those whom they considered worthy: at Bolton the presbyterian elders issued tickets for this purpose. There is no evidence for what went on in the great majority of parishes. Control over the presentation of clergy to livings remained very much in the hands of the nobles and gentry. It is true that where the patron had been the Crown, the bishops, the cathedral chapters or a royalist leader, the power of appointment was taken by the same parliamentary committee which dealt with augmentations. But its members generally took advice from local landowners, including royalists, and only occasionally listened to parishioners, or imposed its choice without reference to local views.[6] From 1646 to 1649 most clergymen entering the Church still went to the deposed bishops for ordination as no alternative means had been clearly established. It is tempting to say of the Church of the Commonwealth that the lack of direction from above encouraged most parishioners and ministers to cling as much as possible to pre-Civil War ways. But the lack of records makes this only an overall impression.

More evidence survives for some of those distinct religious groups which existed either within or without the national ecclesiastical framework. Least need be said about that which had been the most important before 1642, the Roman Catholics. Hated by the Civil War parliamentarians both for their faith and for the support which many of them had given to the royalist cause, they had been savagely punished. Those landed Catholics who had fought for the King lost their estates completely, while those who remained neutral were still deprived of two-thirds. Most had set about recovering their lands by repurchase, but they still had to pay a double share of the national tax upon real estate, and the traditional fines levied upon them for avoiding Protestant worship, levied with a novel stringency. They appeared to be so completely crushed, indeed, that attention was diverted from them for the first time in a century. Instead, it was drawn to those varieties of Protestant who had formed themselves into pressure-groups.

Two of these accepted the notion of a national Church. One consisted of the presbyterians, who between 1645 and 1648 had expected to replace the bishops with local *classes* of clergy and laity whose representatives would determine national policy in synods. During those years such bodies had been established in London and eleven counties, most of them in the south-east or north-west. Parliament intended these to be the first of a nationwide system, but it must be noted that twenty-four counties did not even draw up plans for them, suggesting a lack of general enthusiasm for the project. As soon as Pride's Purge aborted it, no more *classes* were set up and those in existence began to lose membership and some to collapse. Nonetheless, in the capital and in Lancashire, Cheshire and Derbyshire, they remained a significant local force. The other discernible group active within the Church comprised ministers such as John Owen, who were usually called 'independents'. They wished for a much less stringent definition of orthodoxy than the presbyterians, and aimed to level the national body to individual congregations gathered round their ministers, who would meet in national conferences. Their inclination was to limit communion, and perhaps worship, to true believers: some compromised by forming 'inner circles' of 'godly' parishioners who held additional meetings. Relatively few, and found mainly in south-eastern England, these men wielded considerable influence among the leading army officers and MPs.

Outside the Church's boundaries lay the truly independent congregations, of whose political importance, small numbers and doctrinal divisions something has already been said. A few were led by ministers who were prepared to let a national system exist but preferred to remain separate from it themselves. The majority of them rejected the whole idea of a general Church, and their members were nicknamed 'anabaptists' by contemporaries. The name related to the beliefs of the most clearly differentiated sects among them, who reserved baptism to adult believers and were therefore the ancestors of the modern Baptist churches. They divided in turn over the great question of whether humans in general, or only an elect group of them, could achieve salvation. The adherents of the latter view, the Particular Baptists, had formed regional groupings of congregations in the West, the South Midlands, the East Midlands, South Wales and Northumberland by 1653, but all looked to the churches in London for leadership. Those who held the former view, the General Baptists, were also strongest in the capital, with groups concentrated in the Fens, Chilterns and Weald of Kent, all areas of weak gentry authority and long traditions of religious heterodoxy. Both sects together had a total of 54 congregations by 1644, not counting their members in the army, and these multiplied considerably during the next decade. All were voluntary associations grouped around lay preachers who expounded the Scriptures. They were the best-organised of the networks of gathered churches, but there were many other such congregations. Some baptists were included among the Fifth Monarchists, who were not themselves a sect so much as a set of congregations of differing religious beliefs who endorsed the radical political programme outlined earlier. In the years 1648–53 there were also, scattered across the country, many small informal groups who rejected the national Church and met to discuss religion. They had no recognised leaders and could hardly be termed congregations or sects at all. Individuals often wandered between them, seeking ideas. What all these clusters of people had in common, apart from their hostility to the Church of England, was their social complexion. They were drawn overwhelmingly from artisans and small traders, with a few gentry and merchants and some labourers. Yet to say that they were in any way 'representative' even of craftspeople, would be a gross inaccuracy. The combined strength of the different baptist groups in 1653 was perhaps the equivalent of

¼ per cent of the national population. They tended to consist of that minority of the 'middling sorts' of society who had lost faith in the old religious ways and were seriously worried about their personal salvation. What their social and economic position afforded was an opportunity to be more exposed to new ideas than those below them and less worried about the importance of hierarchy than those above.

Certainly, for such people the turmoil of the 1640s, the destruction of assumptions and institutions apparently accepted since prehistory, and the inability of the Commonwealth to establish new orthodoxies, all induced a fever of speculation. Many of them longed for a personal message from the Almighty, and a large number of these thought that they had received one. In 1652 a couple of London tailors decided that they were the Two Last Witnesses of the Book of Revelations. They founded a sect which endured until the 1970s. These 'Muggletonians' aroused little interest in the country at large because they were both cautious and quietist. By contrast a tremendous fuss was raised, both then and since, about the 'Diggers' and the 'Ranters'. The former may be said to have been heralded in 1648 by William Everard, a former soldier and lay preacher, who called upon the poor to support themselves by cultivating the common and waste land of the realm, as communal ventures. But their great publicist was a bankrupt clothier and former baptist called Gerrard Winstanley. His social and political proposals resembled those of the Fifth Monarchists, involving the abolition of the Church, lawyers and universities. But, like some of the 'discussion groups' mentioned above, he had embraced a belief in universal salvation and in the primacy of personal revelation over Scripture. In early 1649 he welcomed the Commonwealth and received a divine instruction of his own, to put Everard's plan into action. By April they had formed a squatter community upon common land in Surrey, while another band, which seems not to have been noticed by historians, occupied the park of the deserted royal palace of Oatlands. Plans were laid by more to camp near Newmarket and elsewhere.[7] Their existence aroused horror in a country which had been accustomed to regard vagrants as enemies and the commons as being for the use of villagers, not interlopers: the Diggers were opposed not so much by the state or by the propertied as by 'straight' society in general. The Oatlands settlement was rapidly evicted by horse troops, probably on the orders of Fairfax, while more soldiers prevented the establishment of the other camps. The Levellers dissociated themselves from Digger ideas. Everard and Winstanley, however, impressed Fairfax sufficiently to have him protect their community, though several soldiers still joined the locals in harassing its members. By early 1650 nine other such squats had appeared, scattered over the counties round London and the Midlands as far as Gloucestershire and Nottinghamshire. They corresponded with each other and two published pamphlets drawing upon Winstanley's arguments. But in April his own settlement was destroyed by irate villagers, and all the others vanished soon after. The leaders of one near Wellingborough were imprisoned by local justices with the approval of the Council of State. Winstanley followed his eviction by publishing a plan for a communist utopia, one of the least influential of his writings in his own age and one of the most important since: though to describe him as 'ahead of his time' is difficult as his vision fits well into a late medieval and early modern tradition of ideal societies and has never been realised yet. Then he retreated comfortably into normality with the aid of a prosperous father-in-law. Within ten years he was acting as a tithe-gatherer and he later became a churchwarden and parish constable. Everard and the others disappeared into obscurity. Most of them were very poor indeed, and the camps were tiny, the largest number recorded at Winstanley's being forty-five. Life in them was even harder than for most paupers of the age. The Diggers matter for three reasons: because of the fuss which they provoked at the time, because of their contribution to the history of ideas, and because they have been much admired by modern radicals. Winstanley, indeed, has the distinction of being the only personality of the period, apart from Oliver Cromwell himself, who has been made the main character of a film.

The questions of posthumous reputation, and of the importance of contemporary reactions, hang still more heavily over the Ranters. They became a *cause célèbre* in 1650, being portrayed in newspapers and pamphlets as a body of people who believed that anybody who made a personal relationship with God was thereafter freed from all moral constraints. Reports of them helped to provoke the Purged Parliament's Blasphemy Act. Recently it has been proposed that they were in fact an invention of the media, an assertion which has given rise to some of the nastiest academic exchanges of our generation. What now seems likely is that they never comprised a group, let alone a sect or a movement. What we have are a series of extravagant ideas and acts associated with individuals who may be identified as members of baptist or other gathered congregations or of no specific religious gatherings at all. In the years 1648–50 we find self-proclaimed messiahs and prophets, preachers who denied all authority but that of personal revelation, people obsessed with the imminence of the Second Coming, others who believed that Christian ethics undermined the sanctity of property, and yet others who were concerned with the liberation of the godly soul from a burden of guilt. There were some melodramatic personal gestures: a woman stripped herself naked during the sermon at Whitehall in 1652 and ran up to the pulpit crying 'Welcome the Resurrection!' Between them, these actions and beliefs can be attributed to only a couple of dozen identifiable individuals. But doubtless they went wider. Cromwell cashiered an army captain for denying the existence of sin, and it seems likely that the ideas described earlier did surface in some of the informal local discussion groups. The mere fact of their existence was enough to horrify many people, whether commoners or MPs, and to inspire the sensational and overimaginative stories in the press. In fact those who shared in this 'moral panic' were facing the wrong way, worrying about incidents in the south of England. They ought to have been watching the dales of the North, where the most important and dramatic popular heretical movement in English history was brewing up, unnoticed by outsiders.

To those at the centre of national affairs, northern England had been a conservative backwater. During the Reformation it was a stronghold of Catholicism, and during the Civil War it had been notably royalist. It was the last region from which large numbers of radicals might have been expected. How it was that they did emerge there has not yet been fully explained, and local research into the matter is much needed. Yet certain factors are clear. The North had many areas where gentry and episcopal influence was weak, where parishes were too large and where tithes were paid to landlords who had bought up the estates of vanished abbeys. The disruption of the Civil Wars and the removal of royalist clergy would have increased the lack of provision or supervision of religion. It was a situation in which the doctrine believed in by Winstanley and some of the informal religious groups, that any visible church was unnecessary and that divine revelation was possible to all humans, could make a devastating impact. In the years 1648–52 this idea was carried through the North and North Midlands by soldiers returning home, wandering preachers and devout artisans and traders in search of fellow spirits. Fresh numbers of discussion groups appeared which believed in it and began to meet more formally, to correspond and to exchange visits. They took over the Fifth Monarchist demands for the abolition of lawyers and universities, but like Winstanley they joined them to a faith in universal salvation and a desire to bring about change by mobilising people in general. By the end of 1652 they were forming an organisation for the purpose of nationwide evangelism. At that date they were scattered over most of the region north of a line drawn between Nottingham and Lancaster. Unlike previous radicals their numbers included many farmers as well as artisans, bridging the worlds of town and country. They were starting to refer to each other as the Friends. Because of the paroxysms which afflicted some when experiencing divine possession, they were becoming known to hostile observers as Quakers.

This, then, was the pattern with which the Purged Parliament had to cope. What local support did it receive in this task? Certainly there were people in the provinces who approved of the Commonwealth. The gathered churches, Diggers and Quakers all expressed loyalty to it, although they differed greatly in what they expected it to do. Groups in County Durham, Berkshire, Bristol and Rye sent petitions against a treaty with Charles I in late 1648, though the latter at least was certainly promoted by an army unit stationed in the town. There were petitions from Somerset and Kent for the trial of the King, and here we have some knowledge of the people involved. The former was the work of a clique led by one very determined JP, John Pyne, while the latter was signed by a variety of individuals in the towns and clothing villages, ranging from fairly wealthy merchants to craftspeople. Many of them were, unsurprisingly, members of gathered churches. A more impressive demonstration of loyalty to the republic was apparently provided in 1651, when Charles II invaded England with a Scottish army. Thousands of militiamen were raised to reinforce the regular army in surrounding and crushing him, and this might argue for a proportionate rallying of feeling to the Commonwealth by this date. Unhappily, as the royal army was being pursued by a superior force, its destruction was very probable, and many of those who enlisted against him may well have been enticed by the prospect of pay and loot. The same problem of material considerations affects our judgement of some activities of the Commissioners 'for the Propagation of the Gospel' in Wales. To pay their itinerant preachers, and to augment the livings of loyal clergy holding benefices, they leased out the tithes of livings seized from bishops, deans, chapters and royalists. This system of tithe-farming survived the demise of the Commissioners themselves. In some places individuals (yeomen or husbandmen rather than gentry) took the leases, while in others the parishioners did so collectively. And yet, again, this cannot be used as evidence for political commitment: it is notable that during the Reformation devout Catholics had bought up confiscated Church property, rather than let Protestants have the lot.

But did the Commonwealth thus create a vested interest in its own survival? Perhaps this question can be better answered by considering the larger one of the fate of the Crown, dean and chapter lands. If they had been distributed amongst many purchasers, would not these people be compelled to support the republic? The answer is that the lands were so distributed, but the people were not so compelled. The first option on purchase of the former royal estates went to their tenants, but few could take it up. Most went to the soldiers whose arrears were to be satisfied by the sale, in lieu of cash. Some were obtained by the leading officers, and some by other ranks who went in for collective purchase. A small proportion was taken by civilians, some of these being members of the Purged Parliament or its local supporters. Of the dean and chapter lands we know less, but the few local studies so far made suggest that a larger proportion, perhaps a fifth or a quarter, was bought by tenants, and perhaps much the same percentage by officials of the Commonwealth. But it seems that half or more were sold to minor gentry from the locality in which the estates concerned lay. In general it might be said that the overall effect of both the sales and the tithe-farming was to enhance the local power-bases of supporters of the regime and to increase the importance of lesser gentry within county society. However, like the tithe-farmers, such landowners were not thereby automatically turned into republicans: rather, they would support another regime if it offered confirmation of their purchases or compensation for them. Overall it seems, once again, that enthusiastic support for the commonwealth was almost confined to the army and to that tiny number of civilians who believed in independent churches. Moreover, many of these were interested in evangelism rather than in entering government. And it is by no means obvious that the Purged Parliament would have given all of them power had they sought it: the MPs disliked many of their own partisans and longed for the favour of more 'respectable' figures who detested the idea of a Commonwealth.

Further light may be shed upon this subject by considering the people whom the new regime appointed as its local representatives. The machinery of county government which Parliament had constructed during the Great Civil War consisted of a web of individuals and commissions. From pre-war days survived the High Sheriff, the Justices of the Peace and the commissioners for the militia. To these Parliament had added a committee in each shire to direct its affairs in general and others to administer estates withheld ('sequestered') from their royalist owners, to purge the clergy and to levy the tax on property, known as the 'assessment'. In some counties all these bodies consisted of much the same people, while in others there were distinctions in membership, notably between the main 'county committee' and the sequestration committee. The central executive organs were also extremely complex, consisting of a mixture of MPs and co-opted members and showing, again, a considerable overlap of personnel. There was the Council of State itself, the committee to fill or augment livings in the Church, another for 'Compounding' (the procedure whereby royalists regained their sequestered estates upon payment of a fine), another to indemnify soldiers for actions committed while on service, others to pay the army and to run the navy and yet more to handle receipts from branches of revenue. Of all these organs, the Purged Parliament only abolished one set, the general 'county committees', while adding a central committee for the taking of accounts. The system of consultation was proportionately complicated. In 1649, the Purged Parliament entrusted its commissioners for the Great Seal with the task of renewing the commissions of the Peace. They were advised in this by the Parliament's own committee appointed to purge or add to the justices, and by the Council of State and the Admiralty Commission, and all these bodies were lobbied by local people. The county commissions for the assessment and the militia regularly proposed new members for themselves to the Council of State, and usually got their way. As the 'general' shire committees were dissolved, it was those for the militia which tended to take over their local importance, and reproduce their membership.

The results of this process, understandably, varied from county to county. Some were placed in the hands of dominant figures, such as John Pyne in Somerset, Sir Michael Livesey in Kent, Robert Bennet in Cornwall, Thomas Birch in Lancashire, William Purefoy in Warwickshire, Wroth Rogers in Herefordshire, Philip Jones in Glamorgan and Herbert Morley in Sussex. Yet no common result derived even from these cases. Pyne and Jones ruled their shires absolutely, but Rogers was sometimes thwarted by other Herefordshire leaders. Bennet, Birch and Jones led cliques of lesser gentry who were new to power, while Morley kept as many important county families as possible represented in local government. Pyne had to reappoint some gentry of dubious enthusiasm for the Commonwealth because he could not find enough wholehearted republicans to fill the posts. In Lincolnshire and Wiltshire there was no dominant individual and a set of lesser gentry took over, while in the Ridings of Yorkshire and in Essex, Hampshire and Devon a list of names from traditional ruling families led the minor landowners brought into government. Almost everywhere under the Commonwealth army officers became more numerous upon the county committees or commissions, but as many of them were also local men their rank was sometimes a false distinction. The offices thus subjected to scrutiny were those which affected security in one form or another, such as that of JP, or membership of the various committees. The position of High Sheriff, being at once onerous and less politically sensitive, was given to men who spanned the spectrum of views, including some royalists. As the Sheriffs appointed the Grand Juries which determined whether people subject to charges should be sent for trial, this acted as something of a check upon the Commonwealth's hold over local justice. Likewise, village offices such as bailiff, constable, tithingman, overseer of the poor and churchwarden, remained open to royalists or to anybody else of sufficient standing in the community: this further limited the impact of the new regime at a local level. In 1650–1 the Council of State delegated to a committee the work of purging urban corporations, using the 'Engagement' as a test, but in practice it removed few individuals. Sometimes the governors of garrison towns would employ their soldiers to enforce the election of sympathetic mayors. In general, however, the municipalities had been cleared of royalists after the Great Civil War, and the Commonwealth was happy to leave these institutions alone unless they contained obvious enemies

The appointment of people to local power by no means meant that they would accept it. This can be demonstrated from the only local commissions which have left copious surviving records, those of the Peace. In all the counties which retain such records, between a third and two-thirds of the JPs named in the Commonwealth's lists of appointees failed to attend the Quarter Sessions. This did not necessarily mean that they did not fulfil any of their duties, for in Devon, the shire where this problem

The Commonwealth

has been most carefully studied, it has been shown that most of
the absentees were active at parish level: they just did not care to
be seen on the Bench with some of the other men named in the
commission. This sentiment was not confined to the most
important gentry included, who might have disliked their new
colleagues as radicals or parvenus, for the minor gentlemen
listed proved just as reluctant to serve. Some absenteeism had
always been a feature of the Bench, but the scale of this was
entirely novel. It increased the already overwhelming tendency
of the Commonwealth's local government to rest upon a handful
of individuals who, from enthusiasm for the Revolution or desire
for office, were willing to serve it. Very few of them were drawn
from the traditional ruling families of each county. Many of the
latter were excluded as wartime royalists or open enemies of the
new regime, and virtually all the remainder refused to act. The
result might be described as a shift of power from the greatest
landowners to the lesser gentry. But, as we have seen, to describe
the social class of lesser gentleman as 'republican' would be
incorrect. It would be wiser to portray the Purged Parliament as
ruling a society divided vertically from top to bottom, with a tiny
minority in each class being prepared to support it actively.
These minorities were slightly larger amongst the middle ranks,
from 'parish' gentry down through merchants and tradespeople
to artisans, but even in these they remained only a fraction of the
total group.

So, if these were the people who ran England and Wales, how
good a job did they do? Were they efficient rulers? Certainly they
faced a very daunting task. All the traditional areas of concern to
JPs, such as crime, the repair of highways and bridges, poverty and
vagrancy and grain shortages, had been greatly worsened by the
wars and the succession of bad harvests which began in 1646 and
continued until 1650. Their workload was multiplied by the transfer of probate and moral offences from the defunct church courts.
The old commissions to raise parliamentary taxation had never
known anything of the weight and regularity of the assessment,
which rated local communities at about 8 per cent of their
presumed income. The pre-war militia commissions had never
faced as formidable a potential enemy as the defeated royalists

39

and their new-found allies now represented. In coping with this web of responsibilities, it must be said that those of the Commonwealth's local commissioners who were willing to serve it did work hard and conscientiously. Famine and destitution were held at bay by the careful administration of the poor law and the distribution of stocks of grain. The worst damage of the wars to bridges and public buildings was remedied. Although the assessment always reached London in arrears, enough of it arrived to ensure that after 1649 soldiers quartered in England and Wales were at last able to pay cash for food and lodging. This was an extraordinary achievement, especially considering that the wars in Ireland and Scotland necessitated the growth of the army from about 30,000 to about 50,000 men between the beginning of 1649 and the end of 1651. There were still gaps in the delivery of money, which officers bridged by using their own resources or borrowing from urban corporations, but at least it appeared more regularly than ever before. The impressive showing of the militia when Charles II invaded had been remarked upon. In brief, the Commonwealth's administration performed the job that it was required to do.

This does not mean that it did not perform it without quarrelling, bungling and corruption. The Council of State was perpetually, and often unavailingly, trying to assert control over the other organs of executive government. The central commissions for the army and the admiralty frequently disputed the extent of each other's powers, and the latter's instructions kept being altered by Parliament. At the local level, committees and commissions sometimes felt neglected by the central government. The Devon sequestration commissioners repeatedly tried to work with the Committee for Compounding in London and as repeatedly failed, because the Committee either ignored or misunderstood them. Some local men accumulated as many revenue offices as possible in order to draw multiple salaries. Some of their colleagues pocketed the revenue itself, and the government had great difficulty in reclaiming the money even when it could be traced. William Bisset was one of the collectors of the Excise, a tax upon commodities, in Wiltshire between 1649 and 1651. At the end of that time he was due to deliver

£1371. Thirty years later the restored monarchy of Charles II, which had inherited all money due to the republic, was still trying to make him disgorge it. In Hampshire a sequestration official helped himself to over £800 and some royalists' goods. Both the Committee for Compounding and the Committee for Accounts discovered this, but managed to recover only a few books from him. The Accounts Committee uncovered a gap of over £1000 between the receipts and payments of the treasurer of the wartime parliamentarian army of Sir William Waller, but each time that it disproved one of his excuses he invented another, until it gave up in exhaustion. Indeed, throughout the period of the Commonwealth this committee remained almost completely ineffective.

As far as the ruled were concerned, did the new rulers behave any differently from the old? Did they represent, as some Victorian writers believed, a 'Puritan Revolution' in morals as well as theology? Or were they, as some Marxists have proposed, the stormtroopers of a new unfettered capitalism, abandoning old paternalist attitudes towards the poor? The toughening of penalties in the Purged Parliament's legislation against sexual offences and profanity would seem to support the first view. But was this legislation enforced? The legal records suggest that the local magistrates and jurymen were too busy struggling with the effects of war and dearth to carry out a 'Puritan Revolution' had they wanted one. Even some of the attempts to reform 'manners' which had been carried out before the wars, such as the closure of unlicensed alehouses, were not resumed on the same scale in most counties because there were so many more pressing problems.[8] In Hampshire, parish officers complained of several hundred such illegal or disorderly establishments, but the Quarter Sessions Order Books record the suppression of twenty-nine. In fact, if there was a campaign to 'clean up' England and Wales, it came from parish level, where the officials had not been altered, and most of the new magistrates could not cope with it. As for the new legislation against sexual misdemeanours, it was apparently considered too savage to be employed upon any large scale. Ordinary people were ready enough to denounce each other, but few of the charges which reached the courts were brought by JPs or constables and the courts were reluctant to convict those accused. So far a total of only four death sentences for adultery have been discovered in the entire country between the passage of the Act of 1650 and its invalidation ten years later. In Devon, the only county where the prosecution of fornication has been properly studied in the same period, only 10 per cent of those who denied the charge were convicted.

What of the treatment of the poor? Here we have two good local studies, of Cheshire and Warwickshire, which have produced identical conclusions. In both counties the attitudes of the new magistrates were more liberal than those who had ruled before the wars. In Cheshire they abandoned the traditional vigilance against vagrants, tried to provide cottages for the homeless and levied a stiffer poor rate. In Warwickshire similar philanthropic efforts were made, accompanied by statements which seem to show a new concern for, and sympathy with, the pauperised. This was associated with a determination to end the long-prevailing underassessment of the rich for local levies. It is possible that the sheer scale of the poverty problem in the late 1640s, and the need to raise large sums, played a part in these developments. Yet it also seems very likely that the lower social status of most of the new justices and the religious zeal of some gave them more sympathy with the middling and poorer ranks of society. Likely, but as yet unproven. And there is, of course, the problem of how far the two counties were typical. In Hampshire the JPs remained very active against vagrancy, and only further research can determine the overall pattern of responses.

Was anything else novel about the behaviour of the republic's JPs? The studies of Cheshire, Warwickshire and Devon suggest that one way in which they made up for the alienation of the traditional ruling elite was to bring people who were not part of that elite further into the processes of government. In all three counties, the Bench began to request reports or surveys to expedite its business from individuals who were not JPs themselves, in a way which would have seemed very odd before the wars. High Constables, parish constables and ministers were favourite recipients of this delegation of authority. In many places the new magistrates had, also, to cope with disrespect upon a scale never experienced by county benches before. In Warwickshire the rule of the Commonwealth's justices was apparently accepted without complaint, but in Cheshire, Devon and Hampshire they were repeatedly derided and disobeyed. Their problem was not that they were thought to be incompetent or corrupt, but simply that many commoners were not prepared to regard them with the respect that had been accorded to the 'natural' ruling elite.

There is one more group in the country at large upon which the impact of the Revolution ought to be considered: the female sex. Was its status in any way affected by the change of regime? From all that has been said of the muted effects of that change upon society at large, the answer might be expected to be negative, and in most ways it is. Not a single group commented upon the fact that all women were barred from either voting for or participating in government: indeed, the abolition of the monarchy removed the sole means which females had possessed of obtaining power, by inheriting the throne. Similarly, no proponents of reform paid any attention to the facts that married women forfeited all property to their husbands, or that women were conspicuously less well-educated than men. As before, female emancipation remained the concern of individual intellectuals, and the principal of these to write in English in the 1640s and 1650s was not a political radical. She was, indeed, Margaret, Marchioness of Newcastle, devoted wife of a royalist grandee. For all this, it must be said that the developments of the 1640s did afford women more activity in public affairs. They had long been prominent in local riots, and this role was extended to take in issues of public concern. In 1642 women enforced the entry of parliamentarian troops to Bristol, in 1645 they led violent protests against the Excise at Derby, and in 1649 thousands of female Londoners demonstrated against the imprisonment of Walwyn, Overton and Lilburne. Many of the gathered churches extended the principle of equality of saints or of universal salvation to afford women an unprecedented part in religious affairs, allowing them to debate, vote and preach within the congregations. It was the Quakers, in this as in all other ways, who took the attitudes of religious radicals to extremes.

They accorded women complete equality at meetings, while during the 1650s almost half the known members of the movement and a little over a third of its roving evangelists were female. Their activity is a reminder that the people of the British Republic found it far easier to break traditional religious boundaries than those associated with politics or society.

III   British and European Affairs

The achievement of the Commonwealth within England was unimpressive, unless the holding operation which central and local government carried out against change and disruption was praiseworthy in itself. Its British achievement, by contrast, was gigantic. Within the four and a half years of its existence it subdued the entire British archipelago. Successive English kings had tried and failed to conquer Scotland, yet now it fell even while Ireland, where previous governments had needed a decade to overcome a single chief, was overwhelmed as well. As part of the mopping-up process which secured the last fortresses in those two realms, units took the remaining English royalist bases in the Isles of Scilly, Jersey, Guernsey and the Isle of Man. How could a regime suffering from such divisions, and so unpopular at home, be so mighty abroad?

Ireland was the first object of its attention, having been designed for an English expedition since the end of the Great Civil War and having in a sense itself declared war upon the Commonwealth. In 1641 most of the island's Catholics had taken up arms to secure safety for their religion, and home rule. Measures to suppress them had been aborted by the English Civil War, which had divided Irish Protestants in turn between royalist and parliamentarian. Parliament's victory in England had tended to drive Catholics and royalists together, while its insensitive treatment of some of its own adherents in Ireland tempted them to defect. Mutual suspicions meant that a coalition between the three groups was very slow to form, but in January 1649 one was completed. Its purpose was to take over the whole realm and then to attack England in the name of

Charles II. It represented the overwhelming number of people in arms on Irish soil, so that the Purged Parliament was soon left holding only Dublin and Derry (or Londonderry). It expected to lose those in turn, but the strength of the new alliance had been overestimated both by itself and by its enemies. The Catholics of Ulster at first refused to join it and suspended operations against Derry. Those of the other three provinces did unite with the Protestant royalists under the King's Lord Lieutenant, James Butler, Marquis of Ormond. They advanced on Dublin, but having no siege artillery they had to settle down to blockade it, strung out on too wide a front. Four regiments sent over from England enabled the governor to punch a hole in Ormond's lines and enforce his retreat. Thus the Lord Lieutenant's forces were already thrown onto the defensive before the main expedition landed from England.

It appeared at Dublin under Cromwell in August 1649, and gave the Commonwealth a total of 10,000 soldiers for the campaign. Now and thereafter, they received regular supplies of food, munitions, money and recruits from England. The fact that their pay was well short of that which was due to them was not important as their arrears would be made up in confiscated Irish land. Cromwell had also brought a superb train of siege artillery, so powerful that when he attacked the town of Drogheda he was able to fire 200 cannonballs at it in one day. The huge new navy built up by the Purged Parliament in the spring drove the royalist fleet out of Irish waters and thereafter dominated the coasts of the island. All these advantages made the Commonwealth's force unstoppable. Ormond disposed of more soldiers, but a decade of constant fighting had left Ireland without the money or food to support a large concentration of troops. Nor were the various regiments in the Lord Lieutenant's coalition used to working with each other. As a result, he dared not face Cromwell in battle, but could only disperse his men to hold key towns which the English cannon broke open. Such a complete loss of initiative added to the already considerable strains with the Catholic–royalist coalition. Many Protestants defected to Cromwell, taking with them important territory including the city of Cork. Their treachery made Catholic towns reluctant to admit Protestant reinforcements, even when this left them almost bare of experienced soldiers in the face of attack. Specific examples of luck (or providence) favoured the Commonwealth, notably that the only capable Irish general, Eogan Ruadh Ò Niall, refused to join Ormond's coalition until late 1649 and then died before going into action. These factors explain how in nine months Cromwell was able to conquer most of eastern and southern Ireland. Thereafter progress slowed because Ireton took over and proved a less skilful commander, because resources were diverted to the Scottish war, and because Irish resistance fragmented into roving guerilla bands which proved hard to catch. But by mid-1653 the whole country was under the Commonwealth's control.

The 'Curse of Cromwell' is still today supposed to be a common Irish malediction. To citizens of the Republic of Eire it signifies subjugation by the English, accompanied by massacres of a quite abnormal ferocity. Is either association correct? The first has much justification, for as we shall see the island became subject to direct rule by the English Parliament for the first time, and much of it passed into the hands of English newcomers. But in another sense the war of 1649–53 was, like all Ireland's conflicts, a civil strife. Both Ormond's forces and those of the Commonwealth were Anglo-Irish. Among the Catholics were most of the descendants of the Norman and English settlers who had seized half of Ireland in the Middle Ages. One of the greatest Gaelic chiefs, Muireadhach Ò Brien, Lord Inchiquin, was a Protestant who had fought for Parliament until thwarted ambition led him to change sides in 1648. Ormond's soldiers included not only many recent English settlers but also royalist refugees from England who had no claim to be Irish in any sense. The whole royalist–Catholic coalition owed loyalty to a King who intended to reside in England as before. The Commonwealth's garrison at Derry consisted of Protestants resident in Ireland before the wars. The same sort of people were included in the force which Cromwell led out of Dublin and many more joined it as it advanced. Cromwell couched his appeals in religious, rather than nationalist, terms. His avowed aim was to succour the Protestants of Ireland and to defeat the Catholic 'rebellion' which had begun in 1641.

What of the massacres? In the summer of 1988 I stopped for coffee at a hotel in Connemara, and watched a promotional video by the Irish Tourist Board. When it introduced the town of Drogheda, it spoke of the time in 1649 when Cromwell stormed the place and killed every man, woman and child within it, as a black day which will live on in the hearts of Irish people for ever. Enquiries in England revealed that this was also the general impression of the events at Drogheda, and at Wexford which the republican army took a few weeks later. These incidents have often been referred to as the great stain upon Cromwell's reputation. But what actually happened? Oliver's instructions were quite specific: to strike terror into other garrisons, he forbade his men 'to spare any that were in arms' within Drogheda. This meant Ormond's soldiers (a lot of whom were English, not Irish) and those of the citizens who were assisting the defence. By the Cromwellians' own account, the latter were quite numerous. But nobody at the time claimed that a single woman or child died, and most of the male population, being unarmed, also survived. At Wexford the same instructions obtained, but some women and children did perish, not at the hands of Cromwell's soldiers but because the boats in which they were trying to escape with their goods capsized, drowning them in the harbour. Perhaps more male citizens were killed than at Drogheda, but more soldiers were spared.[9]

Now, such behaviour was certainly more brutal than *most* of that during the English Civil Wars, but how did it compare with the practice in Ireland? In 1575 the future English naval hero, Sir Francis Drake, called at Rathlin Island, off Ulster, to which the Macdonnells had sent their women and children for safety. He killed all of them and reported this gleefully to his superior the Earl of Essex, who shared his exultation. Yet nobody now seems to remember this 'stain' upon Drake. The Catholic uprising of 1641 began with the greatest massacre of civilians recorded in the history of the British Isles, in which at least 3000 Protestants of both sexes and all ages perished. In 1645 Sir Charles Coote, a Protestant Anglo-Irishman, stormed Sligo, killing the whole garrison and many of the townspeople. In 1647 the Protestant Gaelic chief Muireadhach Ò Brien broke into

Cashel and inflicted the same sort of atrocity upon it. By contrast with all the horror, and with Cromwell himself, Ireton introduced a policy of studious clemency, and sacked two of his officers for brutality towards the Irish. Yet nobody now seems to compliment him for this. I am not attempting to dismiss the suffering of those who died at Drogheda and Wexford. I still cannot motor from the car-ferry port at Rosslare around Wexford harbour without seeming to hear the cries of the drowning women and children. But the fact that it has suited both nations to magnify the actions of Cromwell remains a glaring example of bad history.

To Gaelic writers, the struggle of 1641–53 was *an cogadh do chriochnaigh Eire*, 'the war that finished Ireland'. In one overwhelming sense this was true: it established the 'Protestant Ascendancy' in the land which was to last for 270 years. The confiscations of land to pay the expeditionary force, and to repay those who had lent money to put down the rising of 1641, meant that the proportion of land owned by the Catholics fell from 59 to 20 per cent. When an Irish Parliament met again, in 1661, it had become an almost wholly Protestant body instead of (as until 1641) having an important minority of Catholics. The Norman and English settlers who had arrived during the Middle Ages, and who had run the island for the Crown until the 1530s, suddenly ceased to be a significant political force. As Catholics, they were now treated like their ancestral enemies the Gaels, and began to lose their identity as a group. The much-remembered war of 1689–91 represented only a brief and disastrously unsuccessful attempt to reverse all these developments. In the course of the whole conflict of 1641–53, about 40 per cent of the population of Ireland died (of famine or plague rather than in battle), or fled abroad. The Commonwealth's conquest came after most of the damage had been done, but it added about 15,000 slain in fighting, a few hundreds executed for alleged war crimes, 34,000 encouraged to emigrate to fight for foreign powers, and 12,000 transported or departed voluntarily to the West Indian colonies. This drain of people was not compensated for by immediate fresh immigration from England, because the new Protestant landlords preferred a cowed Catholic population

to newcomers who might expect better terms. The Commonwealth also ended thousands of years of cultural tradition, by
closing the Gaelic schools in which bards were trained. Only the
sheer tenacity of the existing masters prevented the extinction of
their kind, for they maintained the education of pupils informally.
Not only did the century after the conquest furnish some of the
finest of all Gaelic poetry, but the 1650s saw the birth of a
distinctive and beautiful genre, the *aisling* or vision of Ireland.
The old strict metres did give way to freer rhythmical forms,
ridiculed by the great poet David Ò Bruadair as *sraideigse*
(gutter-doggerel), but the new verse proved very effective. All
this, of course, could only with the blackest irony be laid to the
credit of the Commonwealth. Indeed, once the island was
conquered the Purged Parliament and the succeeding regimes
showed every disposition to forget about it. No drive was
launched to convert the inhabitants to Protestantism, although
at this point one might very well have succeeded. As in England,
the episcopal Protestant Church was outlawed but not replaced.
Very few schools were founded, and those were for Protestants.
No opportunity was taken to reform a system of law courts as
overloaded as that in England. No Act of Union was ever passed,
the island simply being declared part of the Commonwealth.
This whole episode illustrates the abiding truth that all that any
English government ever intended for Ireland was to keep it
from being significant.

Throughout 1649 the Scots remained sullenly but passively
hostile to the Commonwealth, allowing it to complete the crucial
first stage of the Irish campaign. The reason for their behaviour
can only be understood in the context of a by then lengthy and
complicated story of Scottish involvement in English affairs. In
the years 1639–40 the majority of the Scottish political nation
had fought two wars against Charles I to secure the establishment in Scotland of a presbyterian national Church, or Kirk,
without any toleration of dissident groups. He had wanted an
episcopal Kirk as close to the English model as possible, but the
Scots defeated him and occupied northern England until he
accepted presbyterianism. When the English Civil War broke
out, it divided Scotland as it had the Irish Protestants. The

majority of those in power allied with Parliament in the hope of securing their new Kirk by having a copy of it imposed upon England. As a result they had not only to send an army into England again, but to fight at home against fellow Scots who believed in the justice of the King's cause. These were eventually defeated, and the army in England made Parliament's victory possible there. Yet the Scots felt seriously let down by their English friends. Not only did the latter try to minimise the Scottish contribution to their success, but (hampered by its own divisions and the attitude of the army) Parliament made slow progress towards establishing an intolerant presbyterianism in England. Almost immediately the Scottish leaders began trying to make an alliance with the defeated Charles to achieve this end, only to find that he, having given up episcopacy in Scotland, would not do the same in England. But by the end of 1647 a majority of the great landowners, and a minority of the ministers of the Kirk, were so worried by the eclipse of Scottish influence south of the Border, and by the growth of independent churches there, that they were prepared to moderate their terms to the King. In return for a promise from him to accept intolerant presbyterianism in England for a trial period, they sent an army south to assist the risings of the English royalists in 1648. This was defeated only because of the follies of its commanders and the brilliance of Cromwell, who then entered Scotland to instal in power those Scottish leaders who had opposed the 'Engagement', the name given to the treaty with the King.

It was this set of men, called by recent historians 'the Kirk Party', which was ruling Scotland at the time of the English Revolution, and although they owed their position to the makers of that Revolution, they nonetheless followed the regicide by proclaiming Charles II King of Scots. This was partly from pique, in that once again their nation had been slighted, this time by the fact that the English had executed their mutual sovereign without any reference to his other realm. The Stuarts, furthermore, were Scotsmen by origin. But the Kirk Party were also the same people who had refused to accept a deal with Charles I which had not guaranteed a permanent presbyterianism in England. They accordingly looked on with intense loathing as the Revolution ensured the continued debilitation of the English Church and the growth of sectarianism. Their problem was that, while they loathed the Commonwealth, they could not come to terms with Charles II. No more than his father would he agree to create the Church that they wanted in England. Instead in 1649 he preferred to set off for Ireland to join Ormond, while ordering the best exiled Scottish royalist general, the Marquis of Montrose, to land in Scotland and to start a rebellion there which might topple the Kirk party. Both projects proved fruitless. The advance of Cromwell in Ireland was so rapid that the royalist cause there soon appeared lost and Charles abandoned his journey thither. Montrose, an adventurer somewhat overrated by modern admirers, reached Scotland only after a long delay and was defeated and put to death. The young King accordingly came to terms with the Kirk Party upon Dutch soil in April 1650, but only as a compromise whereby he promised to confirm the supremacy of its members in Scotland but avoided a commitment upon the issue of English church government. Once he was at sea, the Scottish plenipotentiaries gave him the choice of being abandoned by their government and going back to exile, or agreeing to forsake all his royalist friends, to condemn the alliance made by Ormond with the Irish Catholics, and to impose Scottish presbyterianism upon both England and Ireland. With bitter anger the young King signed this agreement and then served notice that he would revise it at the first opportunity.

Whatever the spirit in which it was made, this pact was an offensive one, aimed at the English Commonwealth, and the latter did not wait to be attacked. Three times in eleven years Scottish armies had crossed the Border, and the English government decided that this time it would launch a pre-emptive strike. Fairfax refused to lead it, overtly because it technically breached former treaties of friendship but probably in fact because it removed the last hope of an accommodation with the King. Instead, Cromwell was recalled from Ireland to command in the new theatre. During the previous December, to reduce its unpopularity at home, the Purged Parliament had cut the assessment by one-third to £60,000 per month. But the new comparative efficiency of collection was maintained, while proceeds were still coming in from the sale of Church land. Added to the other branches of revenue, and the sale of the estates of some leading royalists (most of them irreconcilable exiles), this money provided an invasion force of 16,000 men. It entered Scotland in July.

It faced a much tougher task than that sent into Ireland. Scotland's resources had not been depleted by as protracted a civil war as that suffered by the Irish, the people in charge were not as divided by mutual suspicions and they possessed a capable general in David Leslie. Furthermore, the Scottish government was animated by a unity and zeal of religious purpose and a tradition of victories which the coalition under Ormond did not have. Nonetheless, in a straight fight Cromwell had the advantage. Most of his regiments had existed for years and were used to acting as units, whereas Leslie's force, though containing many veterans, was new-raised. Moreover, the Kirk Party's refusal to employ any officer who was not completely identified with itself meant that many of its commanders were inexperienced. Leslie correspondingly adopted tactics which minimised his weaknesses. He concentrated his army behind a formidable line of fortifications east and south of Edinburgh. The countryside between these and England was stripped of food and every castle in it filled with soldiers. Thus Cromwell spent a month marching up and down the impenetrable Scottish lines while hunger, exposure and disease reduced his army to 11,000. In September he retreated to Dunbar to receive supplies from ships, and was surrounded there by Leslie's army, now 22,000 strong, which was moving in for the kill. The result, instead, was his most dazzling victory. At dawn on the 3rd his soldiers took the Scottish army in the flank as it was awakening, and it was too large and inexperienced to change front to meet them. It was rolled up and routed, losing 14,000 men.

The battle gave Cromwell only Edinburgh and south-eastern Scotland, and the entire winter was required to reduce the castles of this region. But now divisions amongst the Scots played into English hands. The obvious distaste of Charles II for his agreement with the Kirk Party had split the latter between those who viewed his scruples with sympathy and those who wished to abandon him altogether. The second group split away in the autumn to form their own army in the south-west. They were so weak upon their own, and so ineptly led, that an English detachment was able to defeat them and to occupy the area before spring. Thus by the opening of the campaigning season of 1651, the Commonwealth had all of Scotland south of Stirling, the richest and most populous third of the country. Leslie was even less able than before to take offensive, and tried to repeat his tactics of the previous year with a new defensive line stretched across the waist of the country with Stirling in the centre. Behind it the Kirk Party, urged on by Charles, had recognised the folly of trying to limit the war effort to its own proved adherents, and admitted to office former royalists and supporters of the 'Engagement'. This process provided a new army, but one even more hastily raised and unused to working together than that destroyed at Dunbar. Furthermore, its position could be outflanked by an enemy like Cromwell who had himself been strongly reinforced and also commanded the sea. In July he shipped most of his army across the Firth of Forth and seized Perth, cutting off the Scots at Stirling from their supply bases. Charles and most of his officers now attempted the desperate stroke of dashing into England with their army, 13,000 strong, while Cromwell had left the road southward unprotected. Their hope was to spark off a great royalist rising which would topple the Commonwealth while Cromwell was pinned down in northern Scotland by fresh Scottish levies.

The plan was foolhardy, and disastrous. In England the Council of State had held enough soldiers in reserve to seize most potential leaders of such a rising and to patrol the country to cow it. As a result, when Charles's exhausted army settled down to rest at Worcester, only a few hundred English were able to get through to join him. Cromwell, far from being held up, chased the Scots into England after only a week, sweeping up reinforcements as he came. Behind him he left one of the best of his officers, George Monck, with 7000 crack soldiers to continue the pressure upon Scotland. By late August Oliver had surrounded the royal army at Worcester with a force of 28,000, and on 3 September, the anniversary of Dunbar, he overwhelmed the city. Charles himself, as is well known, made an amazingly lucky escape into France after being hidden in an oak tree and various houses. Almost as significant was the fact that virtually no other leader of his army got away. Back in Scotland, Monck stormed Dundee and let his men savagely sack it in order to terrify other towns into surrender. Although many fewer of the garrison and civilians were killed than at Drogheda and Wexford, sixty shiploads of plunder were despatched to England. Monck then captured almost the entire provisional government of Scotland in a raid and, bereft of most of the country's civil and military commanders, the Highland chiefs and most of the remaining coastal towns rapidly submitted. By 1652 only three castles held out, and they had all fallen by May. Scotland was so habituated to loyalty to a central regime that once that regime was removed it found resistance impossible. In Ireland, where authority had traditionally been dispersed, fighting continued for a year after the Scots had given up, even though the Commonwealth had invaded it a year earlier and faced less formidable resistance.

While Scotland was completing its submission and long before all operations in Ireland had ended, the Commonwealth rushed impetuously into its first war with a non-British power. Upon the Continent there was only one notable state which shared the new English government's characteristics of being Protestant and a republic: the Dutch. The United Provinces of the Netherlands were therefore, on the face of things, the natural ally of the Commonwealth, and it might appear remarkable that, instead, the two powers were at war within four years of the regicide. The explanation is rooted in the fact that, unfortunately for both nations, the Dutch and English also shared a third characteristic, of being maritime powers largely dependent upon trade. The United Provinces depended upon it much more heavily than the English, and in the early seventeenth century succeeded in engrossing most of the seaborne commerce of north-western Europe. During the 1620s and 1630s a war between the Dutch and the Spanish gave English merchants the advantage of being permitted into markets from which Dutch merchants were excluded as enemies. But in the 1640s two terrible blows struck English commerce. The first was the outbreak of civil war, the second, and greater, the Hispano-Dutch peace treaty of 1648. The latter allowed the huge Dutch merchant fleets back into every trading sphere and they overwhelmed all competitors. The English had already been driven out of the East Indian spice markets, and during 1649 they lost customers in Spain, the Mediterranean and the West Indies. Informally their response was to fight dirty, by seizing Dutch ships and their cargoes. By the end of 1650 the number gained by this unofficial warfare was already considerable. The formal English response was to negotiate trade agreements, the boldest of all being an offer by the Commonwealth to combine with the United Provinces into a single commercial and diplomatic unit. That such a project could be contemplated is another indication of how ambitious the regime could be abroad even while it was timid in domestic reform. In 1651 the Dutch firmly refused the invitation, and continued to take markets from the English, now especially in the Baltic. In proportion their losses of shipping multiplied, and the Commonwealth now, in petulance, not only continued to ignore these depredations but allowed its own warships to join in them. In the course of 1651 the Dutch merchant marine lost 140 vessels in this manner, and in 1652 the number had already reached 30 by the end of January. In 1651 also the Purged Parliament passed the Navigation Act, prohibiting the Dutch from carrying English goods and so cutting them out of a lucrative freight business. This the Commonwealth offered to repeal only if the United Provinces paid a heavy indemnity. Nobody was much surprised when, in May, the English and Dutch navies opened fire upon each other over an issue of pride, the traditional English demand for a salute from all foreign battleships in the Channel and North Sea. In this fashion both nations blundered into war.

The attitudes to this conflict of individuals within the Council of State and the Parliament are difficult to ascertain. It is known that some of the Neville group, which had articulated a classical republican ideology, were enthusiastic 'hawks', while Cromwell had hoped that negotiation would prevent a breach. But by that May of 1652 nobody in the regime seemed to feel that the war was unnecessary, as so much trade and honour were at stake. There was every prospect, too, of a successful outcome. The superb navy which had been built up in early 1649 had trained by chasing the royalist fleet out of British waters to the Mediterranean, where the King's vessels were captured or dispersed. Overall, the English warships were better made and armed than those of the Dutch, and the latter were weakened also by the fact that their Admiralty was divided between a set of quarrelsome provinces. It was true that the Commonwealth's conquest of the British Isles had left it short of capital assets such as land, but in November 1650 the assessment was doubled, to a record £120,000 per month. New sales of the estates of royalist leaders provided more sums with which to put out the fleet, and it was hoped that the war would pay for itself in the end. The huge size of the Dutch merchant marine, and the fact that the British Isles dominated the sea-lanes leading to its home harbours, made handsome profits from captured shipping likely. Fortified by these beliefs, and by a sense of invincibility fostered by its recent victories all over the British archipelago, the Commonwealth threw itself into the first thoroughgoing naval conflict in English history.

It lasted throughout 1652 and 1653, and to a great extent justified the confidence of its promoters. The English won most of the great battles and their performance steadily improved, as they learned from their enemy first how to fight in line and then how to divide their fleet into squadrons. Some of their commanders proved to be outstanding, notably Robert Blake and George Monck, who had now completed the conquest of Scotland. Their warships generally dominated the waters between England and the Netherlands, and the damage to Dutch merchantmen was indeed heavy. Yet all this did not make the war a success. Despite their defeats, the Dutch kept rebuilding their fleet and renewing the contest. They sent squadrons to the Baltic, Mediterranean and Indian Ocean which wreaked havoc with English trade in all those areas. And, above all, the cost of repairing and supplying the Commonwealth's own navy proved astronomical.

Already by the end of 1652 the seamen's wages were in arrear and victuallers were refusing further contracts unless their existing bills were paid. During 1653 the Admiralty's debts increased to £½ million, and by the autumn unpaid sailors were rioting in the streets of London. The First Anglo-Dutch War had proved to be a bad investment.

Nonetheless, it did play its part in the acceptance of the regicide republic upon the wider European scene. Its conquest of the British Isles, the determination with which it pursued its claims against the Dutch, and the hammering which it gave their hitherto invincible navy, all helped to persuade the Continental powers that the Commonwealth was there to stay and that its friendship was worth having. During 1652 Spain and France both formally recognised the new British state and the Dutch would have nothing to do with Charles II even when he offered to concert a rebellion with their campaigns. By 1653 it was apparent that the only serious threat to the success of the republic would come from its own leaders.

2

THE PROTECTORATE

I   Central Government

The Commonwealth was technically to last for an important eight months after the expulsion of the Purged Parliament. Yet there are good reasons for treating the period from April 1653 until September 1658 as a unit. During that time the army, having failed to obtain satisfaction from the body which it had installed in 1648, embarked upon a series of briefer experiments intended to bring about better results. Furthermore, at the moment that he ordered the MPs from the House, Cromwell turned his already considerable importance in British politics into an absolute dominance which was to last until his death. It is appropriate, therefore, to make at this point an assessment of this remarkable personality, by far the most important and influential in the British Isles during his final decade of life.

Three facets of it will have become plain already: his brilliance as a general, his equal dynamism as a politician, and a certain slipperiness of attitude or tactic which made him all the more effective and dangerous in either role. Until the early nineteenth century he was disparaged more often than praised, but since then the chorus of admiration from historians has been more or less constant. The view that is taken of him in this book is slightly more critical than the norm. So often, the alterations of his politics are described as those of a mighty and divided soul, a conservative country gentleman yoked with a millennarian dreamer. So he was, but he was also a practical politician who yielded to necessities. Repeatedly he would strive for compromise, but as soon as an event appeared inevitable, such as the regicide or the dissolution of the Purged Parliament, he would seize control of the process and so reassert his influence. In the last analysis, he never forgot that his power depended upon pleasing the army. Defenders of Cromwell would suggest that at such times he was waiting to see which way the will of God was tending and then following it. Perhaps he was, but then God clearly always wanted Cromwell to survive politically. Like any politician, he manipulated people and he told half-truths: a reading of his speeches easily illustrates how he remoulded the memory of past events to serve present needs, and altered his persona (squire or saint) to suit his audience. He was by nature expansive, emotional and good-humoured, and employed these attributes as assets, knowing well when to submit others to an outburst of fury, a flight of rhetoric or some boisterous bon-homie. Again, personality and tactic are impossible to distinguish. To say that he aimed at power would be horribly unjust, but he did have a shrewd instinct for retaining it.

The same complex pattern is seen in his choice of clients. As the 1650s wore on, he slowly filled civil and military government with men personally attached to himself. Key army commands went to individuals who had served in his own Civil War regiment. The most favoured were those most closely connected to his own family, his son-in-law Charles Fleetwood and his brother-in-law John Disbrowe. Others among his protégés were former royalists whom he had tempted into his service. The most prominent among these was George Monck, the man who had finished off the conquest of Scotland and then fought so ably at sea. But there were also Roger Boyle, Lord Broghil, son of the Anglo-Irish Earl of Cork, and Charles Howard, one of a prominent Cumberland family. All were unusually talented and all were younger sons, dependent upon public employment to further their fortunes. A third group of clients consisted of his blood relatives, such as his cousins Henry Lawrence, whom he brought into prominence in civil government, and Edward Montagu, for whom he sought a military command. Before long his two sons would be involved in the regime. It has been noted that Cromwell rejoiced in such a heterogeneous following because it represented a union of different backgrounds and ideologies of the sort that he wished for in the nation. It has also been pointed out that he disliked true ideologies, as barriers to this reunion. Perhaps so, but it also suited his practical purposes to surround himself with able subordinates who had nothing in common save their gratitude to him. And ideologues were difficult people with whom to do deals.

In April 1653 many of the consequences of these traits were still in the future, and the pressing concern of the whole army was to replace the Parliament which had just been ejected. Cromwell's action had been so sudden that no contingency plan had been drawn up. A Council of Officers without any fixed membership, chosen by each other, decided upon a new Council of State to administer the realm and a new national assembly to carry out the reforms canvassed since 1649 and to provide for Parliaments thereafter. The Council of State was overwhelmingly military, and the 'Parliament' was, uniquely, to be named by the Council of Officers itself, thereby side-stepping the problem of creating a friendly electorate. The rest of the army was persuaded with some difficulty to accept the decisions of its leaders instead of sharing in their debates, and both councils, of Officers and of State, were riven with discord themselves. But the job was done nonetheless and the nominated assembly called for 4 July. Cromwell's work during this period consisted of trying to foster good relations between the army and the corporation of London, which might provide loans, and of making sure that his own clients got into the new assembly.

The latter convened to a speech of welcome from the general, in which he encouraged it to undertake the work shirked by the Purged Parliament and to satisfy both Fifth Monarchists and presbyterians. This was, of course, an utterly impossible brief. The people who received it numbered 140, and can be called a Parliament only because they formally took the title. If this is recognised, they were at once the smallest Parliament in English history and the first imperial one, for eleven representatives were named to it from Scotland and Ireland (almost all of them

Englishmen serving in those countries). In a sense it was the most representative assembly that England had yet known, having a far greater proportion (two-thirds) of people who were not from the traditional ruling families of their regions. Yet most were not commoners, but minor gentry, and the number who were not landowners amounted to no more than a fifth of the whole. Yet in another sense, of course, they represented only the Council of Officers. Historians have usually called them Barebone's Parliament, after one of the most radical and colourfully-named of them, Praise-God Barebone. As he held no formal position of leadership, and was only a member of a faction, the nickname was a slur. Hence the assembly will be referred to here as the Little Parliament.

It had been chosen to act more speedily than its predecessor, and it certainly did. In the six months of its existence it passed thirty statutes, and many of these were based upon proposals made during the previous four years. The ceremony of marriage was removed from the Church and entrusted to JPs, with registrars elected by the propertied in each parish to record each union. Measures were enacted to relieve both creditors and poor prisoners, and others were proposed to reduce the number of central treasuries, produce a simpler legal code and abolish the most inefficient of the central law courts, Chancery. All this progress, nonetheless, failed to mask divisions more bitter than those known in the Purged Parliament. Repeatedly, the House split between a more radical minority, which wished to abolish tithes, codify the law and abolish Chancery, punish royalists and Catholics and reduce the assessment, and a more 'moderate' majority. The latter were only conservative in relation to the radicals, as many belonged to independent churches, and they included most of Cromwell's clients in the House, including his son Henry, and Montagu, Howard and Disbrowe. They were also drawn slightly more from the greater gentry than the 'radical' leaders, who tended to be lesser gentry or merchants. These 'moderates' won most of the actual divisions, but as winter drew on and some of the less dedicated members slipped away, their majorities began to fall. This was the more significant in that the Parliament was now debating the most emotive issue of all, that of religion. In July it had voted to keep tithes, but in December it called for a bill to abolish the right of patrons to appoint clergy to livings and rejected (by two votes) a plan to have inadequate ministers removed by a central committee. During the same period several of the more 'moderate' members began to wonder about the competence of this Parliament to act as a government at all. It had elected a largely civilian Council of State, which was bungling peace talks with the Dutch. A serious rebellion was spreading in Scotland, while the desire of the 'radicals' to reduce the assessment had annoyed many of the soldiers who might normally have been their allies. Accordingly, some of the 'moderates' decided to destroy the Little Parliament. On 12 December they suddenly withdrew from its chamber and resigned their authority to an amazed Cromwell. Within the next few days a majority of the members gave support to this action, while the minority who remained in the chamber were ejected by soldiers, acting without the authority of the Commander-in-Chief.

It was a feature of this coup, so brilliantly and mysteriously contrived, that a new constitution had been prepared in advance. There was none of the confusion of April, and the successor regime was installed within a week. It had been designed by an individual who thus became one of the most powerful people in the country, John Lambert. Lambert was emphatically not a client of Cromwell, nor of anybody else. He had risen to fame in the North during the Great Civil War, and consistently demonstrated two remarkable talents. One was as a cavalry commander, greatly loved by his men. He had won some of the decisive engagements of the Scottish campaign, making Cromwell's victories possible. The other was as a statesman. He was possibly concerned in the drafting of the *Heads of Proposals*, was prominent in the Council of Officers in April 1653, and was certainly the author of the new *Instrument of Government* which was now enacted. His instinct was to replace the old trinity of King, Lords and Commons with one of King, Council and Parliament, each limiting the others' powers. In discussions during those crowded few days after the 12th, Cromwell and a few trusted advisers amended this blueprint in important respects. A hereditary monarchy and the name of king were both felt to be unacceptable to the army, and so Cromwell was elected as Lord Protector by the new Council of State. His power was greatly limited by the need to consult and to act with that Council, which was dominated by the men who had led the secession from the Little Parliament, and by a list of soldiers of whom Lambert himself was now the most prominent. Its original members held their places for life. This powerful body had not featured in previous proposals for new constitutions, but the projected Parliaments embodied many of the schemes discussed since the *Heads of Proposals*. They were to consist of one chamber, with 400 English members as the *Agreement of the People* had envisaged, plus thirty each from Scotland and Ireland as the Purged Parliament had proposed in early 1653. The franchise was set at the uniform level determined by that Parliament, as was the proportion of county seats (two-thirds). Royalists were barred from voting or standing for nine years, and no Parliament could tamper with the army, the existing religious liberty or the lands confiscated from Crown and State. New elections would be held every three years and the Protector could veto any legislation. The system of checks and balances in the new constitution made it likely that it would be acceptable to anyone who was not a loyal follower of the Stuarts, a Fifth Monarchist or a 'Commonwealthsman' who believed in full parliamentary sovereignty.

Furthermore, it promised to be a reforming administration, carrying out the settlement of the nation that the two successive Parliaments of the Commonwealth had failed to provide. It permitted Protector and Council to issue 'ordinances' before the first Parliament met, and they declared a total of eighty-two in eight months. The 'Engagement' imposed by the Purged Parliament, which had been much ignored in practice, was now repealed. The ordinance involved condemned all such oaths, thereby holding out satisfaction to those sectaries and Quakers who held that Christ's injunction 'swear not at all' applied not only to profanity. Chancery was reconstructed. The Commonwealth's bench of judges was remodelled to remove four men who had been notoriously harsh to royalists, and nearly thirty of the latter were released from prison. During the same period a structure was at last imposed upon the national Church. The plan delivered by the Owen group to the Purged Parliament had been for county committees to examine candidates for the ministry and a central committee to eject those already beneficed who had proved adequate. The scheme was revived in the Little Parliament, and now it was adopted in reverse, with a central board of 'Triers' and local committees of 'Ejectors'. The Triers were a mixture of moderate presbyterians and of men like Owen himself who wanted both a national Church and independent congregations. It even included a few baptists. No common liturgy or doctrine was prescribed, and, of course, the sects were allowed to continue without supervision. Cromwell claimed that only the advice of the Council had stopped him from abolishing tithes. To please all taxpayers, the assessment was at last reduced by a quarter, to £90,000 per month. The hitherto extreme complexity of central government was now tidied up, many committees being abolished or reduced in size, and the revenue system was put under the control of a single Treasury Commission. Several features of the pre-war monarchical administration, such as a Household for the Protector and offices for endorsing documents with a Privy Seal and a Signet, were restored. Much of this was intended to produce simpler and speedier government, but it also provided a symbolic continuity with the old England and Wales which the Commonwealth had lacked.

One problem of a regime which held out something for almost everybody was, of course, that it might satisfy almost nobody. And if it did succeed in earning the goodwill of most of the public, it would still have to reckon with those extremist groups mentioned before, to whom compromise was treachery. Of these, the royalists gave least trouble. Crushed by all their defeats between 1645 and 1651, and offered present leniency and future rehabilitation, the great majority passively accepted the Protectorate. Charles II empowered a group of devoted followers to coordinate conspiracy, but these men, the 'Sealed Knot', had little social or political prestige and in any case were realistic enough to perceive that English royalism was at least temporarily out of

action. Much more trouble was caused by those former allies of
the army who had been infuriated by the events of April amd
December 1653, the 'Commonwealthsmen' and the Fifth
Monarchists. Both sets denounced the Protectorate in word and
print, and five high-ranking officers in the army agreed with
them. That the new government did not suffer badly from these
attacks was due to a mixture of luck and skill. The officers
concerned were scattered across England, Scotland and Ireland,
while the regime's initial measures did indeed appeal to a wide
enough section of opinion to leave its critics isolated. And those
critics were dealt with quietly and ruthlessly. The pattern was
set by the fate of John Lilburne, who returned to England in
1653 after the expulsion of the Purged Parliament, unwisely
presuming that his sentence of exile was now equally defunct.
The Little Parliament promptly had him tried for treason. To
keep to legal forms it allowed him a jury, and as in 1649 he was
acquitted. This time, however, the Council of State failed to
release him, and when Cromwell took power Lilburne was
transferred to an island prison, and died in captivity. The army
officers who objected to the Protectorate were all swiftly
cashiered or allowed to resign. Along with the regime's other
vocal opponents, they were hauled before the Protector and
Council for a warning, and if they persisted in their defiance they
were bundled off like Lilburne to remote fortresses. It has been
suggested that Cromwell and his councillors were thereby being
merciful, by avoiding trials which would have cost these men
their lives and providing the option of releasing them when they
calmed down (which happened to several). Perhaps so. But this
method was also a remarkably effective way of removing critics
with the minimum of publicity and in breach of the most
elementary rules of justice.

To substantiate its claims to legitimacy, it was essential that
the Protectorate call a Parliament swiftly. It also needed one to
obtain a grant of money. The Purged Parliament had not only
consumed a huge amount of capital assets in the shape of
confiscated land, but spent £1 million more each year than it had
earned. The continuation of the Dutch war through 1653, and
the Protectorate's cut in the assessment had worsened the debt,

to the extent that nobody was now willing to lend money to the government. The latter did make peace with the Dutch, but still spent £350,000 more than its revenue during 1654. So a Parliament was called, under the new constitution, for 3 September. Few of the Purged Parliament's members, or of the radicals from the Little Parliament, were returned to this one, while enough of the Protectorate's own members and clients were there to form a significant government interest. The bulk of those elected were the sort of gentry whom Pride's Purge had been designed to remove from power, Civil War parliamentarians who would never have supported the regicide. Cromwell's welcoming speech was therefore aimed deliberately at the political middle ground, calling for healing and settlement and lambasting the Levellers, Fifth Monarchists and Ranters. To his horror, the Parliament immediately set about debating the legitimacy of the *Instrument of Government*. The tramp of jackboots was heard again: on the 12th the MPs learned that their House was guarded by soldiers instructed to admit only those who agreed to accept the fundamentals of the constitution.

This got rid of the true Commonwealthsmen like Hesilrige, but the Parliament that remained showed itself very ready to redefine the details of the constitution in a way that Protector and Council found disturbing. Upon two enormous issues the government and the majority of the members slowly drew apart. One was that of religious liberty which most of the MPs believed had become too extensive. They wanted both a doctrine for the Church and a curtailment of the freedom which had been granted to dissenters. The other was the matter of money. From the beginning, the MPs were only prepared to vote an assessment cut by another third, on the understanding that the army would be reduced in proportion. The total financial establishment which they proposed for the regime seemed to its leaders to be quite inadequate to its needs. On 20 January 1655 the Parliament began to discuss the formation of a militia which might replace many of the army's functions, and resolved to deny use of this body to Protector and Council without a Parliament's permission. Two days later they were summoned before a furious Cromwell, who accused them of fomenting discord and dissolved them.

The fate of the First Protectorate Parliament left the status of the *Instrument of Government* in doubt. On the one hand the Parliament had never finished revising it, and so it had never received legal endorsement. On the other, most of the same MPs had agreed to accept its fundamentals, and it suited the Protector and Council too well to be scrapped. So they set about measures designed to induce the next Parliament to be more co-operative. Initially, these were aimed to conciliate the sort of people whom the last one had represented. A proclamation was issued to restrict religious liberty, to the extent of ordering the punishment of dissenters who disturbed the services of the national Church. The assessment was cut as the Parliament had wished, to £60,000 per month, and the total size of the army in the British Isles was brought down from 57,000 to 40,000 men. The soldiers' pay was also reduced, but as harvests had improved and food prices were now less than half what they had been in 1649, this proved acceptable. Even as these measures were being enacted, however, the same government was setting about others designed to show the nation that it would deal savagely with extra-parliamentary opposition. The occasion of these was a tragi-comic royalist rebellion on 8 March. It was the product of two sorts of desperation. One was that of Charles II's exiled court, which was now living upon the charity of German states and needed to remind Europe that his cause was still alive. The other was that of a group of royalist hotheads, socially and politically insignificant even in their own party, who were tired of the caution of the Sealed Knot and longed for action. Charles made matters worse by failing to give a clear mandate to his adherents in England either to rise or to wait for a better opportunity. The Protectorate now possessed a patchy but very active network of spies and informers, and had enough intimation of the plotting to arrest many potential leaders. As a result, when the signal for rebellion did come it was obeyed only by tiny groups, all but one of which dispersed as soon as it had gathered and realised its weakness. The exception was in Wiltshire, under John Penruddock, and that was chased into Devon and rounded up by a single horse troop.

This episode should have left the government feeling secure

and confident. Instead it exasperated the Protector and Council and roused them to some very dirty work. They employed trial by jury against Penruddock's band, as the offence of most of these men was obvious enough, and executed only twelve out of the thirty-three found guilty. But they then transported to the West Indies not only all the rest who had been condemned but those who had been acquitted and some who had not yet been tried. The whole body of people who had been engaged in royalism since 1642 were now declared to be under suspicion, although they had so conspicuously failed to support the rising. The wealthier among them were instructed to pay a 'decimation tax' upon their property, for the upkeep of a new militia led by local supporters of the Protectorate and intended to watch them. Furthermore, they were forbidden to come near London, sanctions were tightened up against the use of the old Prayer Book, and any clergy ejected from the Church since 1642 were barred from taking posts as private chaplains or as schoolteachers. In August ten (later eleven) of the leading men in the army were commissioned as Major-Generals, each to supervise a different set of counties. Lambert, Fleetwood and Disbrowe were amongst those so empowered, and they were instructed to improve local government and to reform morals in their areas as well as to provide complete security. Seven months after Cromwell had accused a Parliament of encouraging disunity, his government had wrenched open the divisions of the Great Civil War. The surviving evidence does not permit us to explain such an enormous over-reaction, or (though Lambert has often been named) to identify the moving spirits behind it.

In other respects also, the Protectorate behaved more roughly from the spring of 1655. In May it tried a merchant called Cony, who had refused to pay customs dues to a regime which had no legal basis. Cony could, of course, not be allowed to win his case, but the methods used to cow him disturbed even some who had hitherto loyally served the Protector. They consisted of the simple device of sending to prison all three lawyers who undertook to act for the defence. In June Cony gave up. One of the judges resigned in protest at this behaviour, and at the same time (as described earlier) four others were dismissed for casting doubts upon the validity of the regime or its actions. They were replaced by more compliant individuals. More former allies of Cromwell and his councillors criticised their actions and were interned without trial. The Secretary of State, a clever client of Cromwell called John Thurloe, was given not only an enlarged espionage system but also powers to censor the press. The Protector himself claimed, as in the case of tithes, to have had the decision imposed upon him by his Council. This may well have been true, but whatever its origins the measure was certainly well enforced. Within a few months the only news-papers to appear regularly were the government journals edited by the timeserver Marchamont Nedham, who had fulfilled the same service for the Commonwealth. But Nedham's style had changed. In the days of the Purged Parliament he had written vivacious, witty propaganda. Now he made his papers as tedious and barren of news as possible: it is a feature of authoritarian regimes that they try to destroy the interest of the ruled in the activities of their rulers. *The Instrument of Government* allowed Protector and Council to issue ordinances only until their first Parliament met. Now they issued 'proclamations' instead, for which there was no legal warrant even by the increasingly dubious authority of the *Instrument*. They compounded the impression of arbitrariness by employing a proclamation to limit the eligibility of people to sit in municipal corporations. The Purged Parliament had only tried to exclude royalists, but the Protectorate now theoretically restricted membership to the 'godly', which apparently meant whatever the government wished.

Nonetheless the Protector and Council followed up these steps with less energy than their pronouncements suggested. The local impact will be considered later: for now it is sufficient to note two developments. First, that once on their beats the Major-Generals were more or less ignored and their constant requests for advice and encouragement went unanswered by the Council or the Protector. Indeed, Cromwell himself was often absent from important Council meetings: whatever his talents as soldier and politician, he was not an administrator. The second develop-ment was that the regime drew back from the crucial step of imposing taxes without a Parliament. Taxes were certainly needed, for not only had the reduction in the army not been sufficient to compensate for that in the assessment, but a new naval war had broken out with Spain. The decimation tax proved inadequate to pay the new militia, and Cromwell and the Council were unwilling to accede to the proposal of some of his Major-Generals, to lower the threshold of the property liable to it. By early 1656 annual expenditure was outrunning income by £230,000 despite many economies. The options were to extend the decimation tax to non-royalists or to try another Parliament. Cromwell claimed later that he was pushed into the latter course by the Major-Generals, but the evidence in Thurloe's papers makes this claim rather dubious. Certainly, there were protracted debates about the matter in the Council before a Parliament was called, for 17 September.

Most of the Major-Generals were confident that they could get good men into the House. But then, the greatest strength of the regime lay in its ability to exclude, not include, MPs. According to the *Instrument*, the latter were required only to be of 'known integrity' and not royalists. The Council was by now, however, used to breaking its own rules and altered this to 'integrity to the government'. About a hundred members were thereupon excluded from the House, and as more withdrew in sympathy, this process removed in total about a third of its number. The remainder consisted, by and large, of the sort of individuals who had sat in the previous Parliament. But this one was to be different, characterised not by a struggle between the government party and the backbenchers so much as by a division between the supporters of the regime themselves, over three great issues. The first was religion, embodied this time not in debates over the form of the Church but over the fate of a Quaker leader, James Naylor. More than any other group, the Quakers had called the bluff of the Protectorate's religious settlement. The latter was intended to allow the existence of godly and peaceful nonconformists, who might contribute useful ideas and experiences to each other and the national Church. The Quakers were undoubtedly pious, and their sincerity was only too appallingly clear, but their missionary activity depended upon confrontation, abuse and dramatic individual gestures. Cromwell himself clearly did not quite know what to make of them, finding their leaders impressive if in some respects deluded. In personal interviews he treated them gently and warily, and he obtained the release of some of them from prison. But he also encouraged the weeding out of their converts from the army and from local government and punished one who challenged the preacher in his own chapel. How little his restraint was shared by some of his own followers was revealed when Naylor was brought before the Parliament in December 1656. He had been arrested at Bristol for staging an entry to the city in the manner of Christ, and only the supreme tribunal of the land was felt to be worthy of dealing with the enormous implications of the action. His appearance permitted an explosion of feeling from all those members who believed that the existing religious liberty was too ample, and it completely shattered the government group. Some of the Protectorate's military leaders, such as Lambert and Disbrowe, and some of its civilian councillors, argued for clemency. Others among the regime's members and supporters wanted Naylor put to death. In the end the Parliament did not choose either option, but decided to have the wretched man flogged, branded, preached at and imprisoned. The case deeply worried Cromwell, who demanded to know by what authority the MPs had acted and got no answer (the true one being that they acted as the entire Protectorate did, by expedient). Perhaps he regarded the process as a danger to his own powers, or perhaps he personally deplored the savagery of the punishment, or perhaps he feared that the gathered churches would begin to feel threatened and domestic instability would increase. Whichever combination of these reasons applied, he could not have been pleased by the disagreement among the ranks of his own followers.

On the day that the Protector sent his message about the unfortunate Quaker, the second great divisive issue surfaced. Disbrowe presented a short bill to lend legal foundation to, and to continue, the decimation tax. He expected it to pass quickly, and was surprised when it became the subject of weeks of debate. The tax was repeatedly attacked as unjust and divisive and on

29 January 1657 it was rejected by thirty-six votes. What especially infuriated the Major-Generals was that they had been opposed by civilian clients of Cromwell such as the Anglo-Irishman Broghil, and by quite obscure relatives of the Protector who would not have acted without his countenance. Indeed, Cromwell himself ignored the soldiers' appeals to intervene upon his side, and gave a rich cloak to a cousin who had condemned the tax. Its abolition meant the end of the new militia, and of the Major-Generals, and the latter suspected (quite reasonably) that the Protector had sacrificed them in the hope of conciliating the Parliament and so bringing about a lasting settlement. If so, it was a gesture which promised some success, because the next day the MPs voted the government £400,000 towards the Spanish war.

In fact, people such as Broghil were aiming at something far more ambitious than the end of the Major-Generals' rule: they intended to reconcile the whole nation to the Cromwellian regime by turning it into a monarchy on the pre-war model. On 24 February they suddenly proposed to the Parliament that Cromwell be made King, and the governing team of the Protectorate became apparently hopelessly divided over this new issue. Most of the civilian councillors, and the judges, supported the proposal, whilst most of the soldiers, led by Lambert, opposed it. Lambert himself had apparently been happy to crown Cromwell in 1653. What distressed him about the new initiative was that it was the work of a clique which had nothing to do with the army and which clearly intended that, for the first time since 1648, the running in politics was going to be made by civilians. And it was soon obvious that more than monarchy was aimed at, for that suggestion was followed by others for an Upper House to the Parliament and (once more) for a doctrine to be prescribed for the national Church. The army reacted immediately: four days after that first motion for monarchy, Lambert led the former Major-Generals and a deputation of officers to complain to the Protector. This time, they were going to make sure that he weighed in to support them, as he had not done over the decimation tax. Instead, they encountered all the force of personality which had carried their commander to the summit of the nation. He accused them, furiously, of having failed to settle the country for four years, exempting himself from any part in that process. He then told them that a final settlement at last seemed possible, and that a second chamber to Parliament might have saved James Naylor. The performance was a magnificent one, and partly successful. It did not convince some of the officers, including Lambert, but it made enough of the others hesitate to permit the debates in Parliament to go forward. The Protector became the target of intensive lobbying, as many of the gathered churches, terrified of any backward step from the Revolution which had guaranteed their survival, added their pleas against kingship to those of the soldiers. Against them were now ranked most of the Parliament and of the Council, who pleaded with equal determination. What happened next is too often explained (like so much else) in terms of the Protector's psychology and beliefs, his instinctual reaction against the title of King because it was precisely the sort of vanity to which his God had so often seemed hostile. The sequence of events indicates that more practical considerations ought, at the least, to be credited with some importance. On 6 May Cromwell at last informally expressed his readiness to accept the Crown, and this aroused the army to a last desperate effort. Lambert, Fleetwood and Disbrowe, the three greatest men in it, all told the Protector that they would resign if he carried out his intention. Then Cromwell heard that Pride, the colonel who had presided over the purge in 1648, had raised a petition against monarchy from most of the regiments in the London area, and was taking it to the Parliament. It had been drafted by John Owen, the churchman who had had so much influence in the early years of the Protectorate. This impending, possibly calamitous, confrontation compelled Cromwell's decision: on the 8th, as the petition reached the House, he removed the need to deal with it by absolutely refusing the Crown.

The result was a compromise, whereby a disgruntled Parliament accepted the Protector's decision against kingship and an unhappy army accepted all the other proposals agreed upon by the MPs. The latter were, however, reinterpreted by Cromwell and his councillors. Although the Protector remained without the title of King and a crown, he was now enthroned for state occasions, with a royal robe and sceptre. An Upper House of sixty-three members was added to the Parliament, but it consisted not of the traditional nobility but of individuals named by Cromwell. The overwhelming majority, of course, turned out to be his friends and clients. The Protector agreed that a doctrine would be defined for the national Church, by an assembly of divines, and then failed to call such an assembly. He vetoed a bill intended to prosecute anybody who failed to attend the Church's services without presenting a certificate from a minister of an independent congregation. He did accept a savage new law against Catholics, making possible the confiscation of two-thirds of the estates of each one, which nobody then enforced. The chief weakness in the package concerned the revenue. In April the Parliament voted one of £1,900,000 per year, with an extra £400,000 per year until the Spanish war ended. It did not, however, agree upon how to raise all of this, and ignored Cromwell when he pointed out that the armed forces alone currently cost almost £2½ million per year: like the First Protectorate Parliament, the second one did not believe in as much armed force as the Protector did. What it did do was to reduce the assessment still further, to £35,000 per month. Thus, the MPs had effectively done everything except to perform the task for which they had been called together. Nevertheless, the country now had a new constitution, called the *Humble Petition and Advice*. Its net result was to enhance the powers of Protector and Parliament slightly at the expense of the Council. The latter lost the ability to choose Cromwell's successor and to determine whether or not war should be declared (both of which went to Cromwell) and to purge MPs (which was left to Parliament). The crucial issues of who controlled the armed forces or finances were (of course) left undecided. Nonetheless, the *Humble Petition and Advice* did possess a legitimacy, as a decision of Parliament, which the *Instrument* had lacked. This did not necessarily mean that it would work.

For the rest of 1657 Cromwell thought that it would. In June he sent the Parliament into recess, with gratitude and praise. The only damage done to the government team as a result of the whole political contest of the spring was the dismissal of Lambert. For over three years he had been the second most important person in the Protectorate, a position marked by such symbolic roles as carrying the sword of state before Cromwell on ceremonial occasions and riding with him in his coach to the opening of Parliament. Had the Protector died during that period, Lambert would almost certainly have been chosen by the Council to succeed him. Now he could not forgive Cromwell for the destruction of the *Instrument of Government* and his own loss of influence, and refused to work within the new constitution. The Protector deprived him of his offices, showing little dismay, and thereby turned the Council almost wholly into a body of people who had owed their place in public life to his favour. Into Lambert's place in the regime he promoted his own elder son Richard. Until this point he had deliberately neglected to prepare this young man for any role in politics or war, apparently for fear that this would be taken for a sign of ambition upon his own part. Now, with the tide of opinion apparently running so strongly in favour of a Cromwellian monarchy, or quasi-monarchy, Richard Cromwell was plucked out of an obscure existence as a Hampshire squire, and given the honours due to a prince. John Owen was punished for his part in the affair of the army petition by being dismissed from his post as Vice Chancellor of Oxford University.

On 20 January 1658 Oliver Cromwell remet the Parliament with a confident speech of welcome. He appeared to have forgotten that under the terms of the *Humble Petition*, the Lower House could now be purged only by itself. So, over a hundred hostile MPs were now back in it, while the government had lost about thirty of its best speakers by promoting them to the new Upper House. The Protectorate's enemies at once challenged the legitimacy of that second House. A prolonged debate followed, and an appeal from the Protector, to pay attention to the government's needs, provoked no response at all. Worse, the Commonwealthsmen had perceived in the reactions of the army to the prospect of monarchy a year before, an opportunity to subtract the loyalty of the soldiers from the Protectorate. They prepared a petition which linked the resumption of absolute authority by the House of Commons, the guarantee of a very wide toleration of religious belief and an undertaking that no members of the army could be cashiered without a proper hearing before a court martial. The further cut in the assessment in 1657 meant that since 1654 it had been reduced by more than half while the size of the army had been reduced by less than a third. The soldiers' pay was now six months in arrear, and it is likely that some of them were genuinely worried by the mildly reactionary character of the *Humble Petition*: for whichever reason, some regiments began to get restless. Cromwell panicked, more severely than he had done over the petition in May 1657. He forestalled the delivery of this one to the Parliament by dissolving the latter, only two weeks after it had remet. He then called together all the army officers in London, to appeal to them for loyalty. All gave it except the six from his own horse regiment, old comrades from the Civil Wars, who condemned the *Humble Petition* and were promptly cashiered (without court martial). Fleetwood, technically the senior officer in the army under Cromwell himself, now worked hard to obtain an address of obedience to the new constitution from the soldiers in England. He succeeded, and a personal appeal from the Protector produced another from the Corporation of London. With this, the crisis passed.

Its consequences were less easy to deal with. After more than four years of existence, the Protectorate had still not managed to make a working relationship with a Parliament. It had just bound itself within a new constitution which apparently did not work, and an atmosphere of the provisional and the unstable still surrounded the regime. In May another madcap royalist plot, work of a few hotheads, was uncovered. A new High Court of Justice, without a jury, was commissioned to try those arrested, and this time all but one of the judges refused to sit in it. It was filled up with other lawyers, and executed five men, but the legality of the procedure was even more patently dubious. With each month the revenue slid deeper into deficit and the pay of the armed forces further into arrear. What was needed to remedy the problem was a massive increase in taxation. Most of the Council agreed that without a Parliament this was not politically feasible, and it seemed unlikely that a Parliament would grant it. The councillors had never quite forgiven each other after the rift which had opened among them over the issue of kingship. The military leaders Fleetwood and Disbrowe remained deeply resentful and suspicious of some of the civilians. Disbrowe expressed his contempt for Richard Cromwell, the heir apparent to the Protectorate, who had little knowledge of politics and none of war. It was becoming obvious that Oliver Cromwell's habit of surrounding himself with people of such differing views and backgrounds meant that they could not work together once his leadership was removed. And that leadership was faltering.

The great Protector had never been a statesman. Throughout his career the main political initiatives had been created, the constitutions drawn up, by others. His genius had been to execute them, and to inspire those involved in the process. Once everybody else was out of ideas, Cromwell was the last man to provide any. After his great effort to save his regime in early 1658, he lapsed into a torpor which became terminal. Repeatedly, his Council failed to agree upon whether to try another Parliament or to impose a tax without one. Repeatedly, it waited for the Protector to make a suggestion or to take a decision, and none was forthcoming. As the summer drew on, it became obvious that the disappointment of the spring had not just stunned Cromwell, it had broken him. His health had been vulnerable for years, especially at times of pressure, so that he had been ill during a long part of the Scottish war and during the kingship crisis of 1657. In mid-1658 he gave observers the impression of being a sick man, long before any physical disease settled upon him. His handwriting turned into that of a geriatric, and when a fever did take hold of him, in August, he showed little will to live. On 3 September, his own birthday and the anniversary of the victories at Dunbar and Worcester, a tremendous storm broke over England. When it had passed, the life of the Lord Protector had gone also. In many ways his tale, like that of his great opponent Charles I, had been a tragedy. Both men had sincerely wished the best for their country, and viewed all of their actions to which others took exception as necessities. Cromwell certainly may be credited with more ability to distinguish between his country and himself and to recognise that the necessities might be regrettable. But there is a well-known proverb about the way that is paved by good intentions, and the inventions mothered by necessity are commonly crimes.

II   The Localities

At first sight, the relative instability of central politics between 1653 and 1658 was balanced by a relative stability and continuity of local government. The provinces were the scene of far less confrontation and upheaval than Westminster, and it is tempting to suggest that away from all the drama in the metropolis life went on smoothly and peacefully, with the processes of governing carried on efficiently enough. There would be a great deal of truth in this portrait, yet the parallels are as striking as the contrasts. In both spheres there was no great change in the identity of the people who performed the executive tasks of the Protectorate, but they worked in an atmosphere of constant tension and anxiety, confronted with a perpetual and apparently insoluble problem of gaining active cooperation, instead of sullen obedience, from most of the ruled.

So who were the people who ran the provinces for the Protector and Council? As before, it is difficult to provide a general answer. It would be true to say that during the time of the Little Parliament radicals from the minor gentry or non-landed classes tended to be added to the commissions for the peace and the 'assessment'. And that under the Protectorate individuals of more 'moderate' beliefs and of higher social status tended to be put in. It would also be true to say that probably neither of those statements applied to the majority of English and Welsh counties. In Hampshire, the Ridings of Yorkshire, Cumberland, Westmorland, Cheshire and Leicestershire, there was little alteration in the ruling teams bequeathed by the Purged Parliament. In Herefordshire, Cornwall, Kent and South Wales, the 'county bosses' switched allegiance smoothly with the changes of central regime and increased their local power. In Sussex Herbert Morley refused to serve in central government after the ejection of the Purged Parliament, but he remained an important figure in county affairs. In Somerset John Pyne flatly refused to serve the Protectorate in any capacity, and so his whole clique lost control of local government. It was replaced by an increasing number of gentry of moderate views and from wealthy families, including some sons of royalists. In North Wales and Lincolnshire likewise, some of the main parliamentarian gentry returned to the bench in the late 1650s. In Buckinghamshire the fall of the Purged Parliament enabled a group of religious radicals to seize control of the county, and a few of the same sort of individual were added to the commissions of some other shires. But the demise of the same Parliament also allowed the restoration of four justices of notably moderate views to the Warwickshire bench. In Surrey, the Protectorate elevated the Onslow family, part of the traditional county elite, to local dominance. In Devon it at first both retained the radicals added in the time of the Little Parliament and called back prominent supporters of the Purged one. But later it dropped half the radicals and some of the Commonwealthsmen, substituting wartime parliamentarian gentry who had been displaced at the Revolution. In Wiltshire the decisive change happened months before the fall of the Purged Parliament. In 1649 a drastic purge had placed power in the hands of a set of political and religious radicals, a mixture of minor gentry and commoners. Then in 1652 a number of these men were replaced by some of the parliamentarian gentry removed in the purge, and by new-comers of more 'moderate' views, and this balance endured for the rest of the decade.

So can any overall conclusion be drawn from these case studies? Really only one: that the Protectorate, like the Commonwealth, used almost anybody who seemed prepared to support it. The result in both cases was a patchwork of county administrations, containing varying proportions of greater and lesser gentry, merchants and tradespeople. The fact that the Protectorate's commissions contained slightly more of the traditional elite indicates that it had slightly more potential to satisfy that elite. But three large additions must be made to that last statement. First, that no more than a fraction of the nobility and greater gentry of England and Wales were still either allowed or prepared to serve the regime, so that the economic and social rulers of the country mostly remained outside the power structure. Second, that no more than under the Commonwealth did inclusion in a commission indicate readiness to serve. In January 1654 seven out of eighty-two people listed in the Hampshire and Southampton assessment commissions turned up to launch the year's work. Mercifully for local administration, it tended to be the most experienced and active justices who survived the changes. In Somerset almost half the bench which had served the Commonwealth had been replaced by the death of Cromwell, but less than a third of those who actually turned up to Quarter Sessions. In Dorset only three of the regular attenders of the Sessions were put out of commission between 1650 and 1659. Continuity in the East Riding of Yorkshire was provided by thirteen JPs (out of eighty-one in the various commissions) who served throughout the Interregnum. These equivalents of local bureaucrats tended either to come from the pre-war elite or to have family connections with it. To some extent, purges were a function of old-fashioned gentry feuding, and the justices or assessment commissioners who were dismissed were often clients of local notables who themselves remained in office. The fact that the idle or the unimportant were the normal victims of changes in personnel explains much of the steady work of local government throughout the period.

There remains, however, a third rider to the statement that the Protectorate was slightly more acceptable to traditional local rulers: that property-owners as a whole would not, given a free choice, have selected the Protectorate's appointees to govern them. This may be illustrated very easily from parliamentary elections. The *Instrument of Government* had followed the intention of reform proposals since 1647, of creating a more independent electorate, less amenable to manipulation by either local magnates or the government. This lay behind the substitution of so many county seats for borough seats. It was an example of how a genuine idealism upon the part of those who made the English Revolution clashed with the realities of their situation. For they were, of course, now the government whose manipulation of elections was being weakened by the reforms. In practice, the Protectorate got its most important figures, such as councillors and leading army officers, into Parliament as easily as the old monarchy had done, for local communities were usually happy to elect powerful people who would show suitable gratitude. But the bulk of the MPs returned to both the Protectorate Parliaments were considerably more socially prestigious and considerably less devoted to the regime than the individuals whom the government had put in charge of local government. Doubtless they would have included royalists if these had not been specifically excluded by law. As it was, the lack of an electoral register meant that many of the King's adherents turned up to vote, regardless of the fact that this was also prohibited. This made the success or failure of the Protector and Council to come to terms with those Parliaments all the more significant. In 1657–8 it seemed that real progress was being made to establish the regime at a local level, as the *Humble Petition* seemed to be doing at the national one. It was during these years that substantial county gentry were returned to the commissions of the peace and assessment in Somerset, Devon, Lincolnshire and North Wales, and also that attendances by justices at Quarter Sessions were generally higher than at any time since the regicide. But this achievement was no more than a beginning.

Such a portrait also ignores the very important role of the army in the localities. Every local commission, and the local revenue collectors, included a percentage of officers currently in service. They also acted as sheriffs. By this means the regime filled gaps left by a lack of local civilian collaborators and provided individuals who, if necessary, could drive on county government. Already significant under the Commonwealth, this practice increased under the Protectorate, until in 1658 there were more soldiers in the commissions for the peace and the assessment than ever before. Thus, the local government of the Protectorate became more military even while it became more socially respectable: a typical Cromwellian paradox. But then these officers were just one facet of a considerable military presence in the provinces. The coasts, Wales and the Welsh Marches were full of garrisons. London always contained five or six regiments, while detachments of horse were quartered in a wide ring around it and close to the main towns of the Midlands and the West. The obvious question to ask about this situation is how cheerfully civilians put up with it. The answer (yet again) is that responses varied between districts. In counties such as Kent and Hampshire, which were long accustomed to fortresses and convoys, there seems to have been little tension. Everywhere the money spent by soldiers must have stimulated trade. Some military governors, such as George Fenwick at Berwick or Thomas Kelsey at Dover, made notably good partnerships with the corporations of their towns. Army officers were sometimes themselves local gentry, although minor members of that class, and colonels or governors who were new to a region sometimes became important local figures in it. There is no real evidence in the time of the Protectorate that civilians *en masse* objected to soldiers as such. On the other hand, some civilians objected very much to what particular soldiers did. The great misdemeanour of certain garrisons, in the eyes of the corporations and citizens whom they were theoretically guarding, was to promote religious radicalism in the community. At Exeter, Hull, Poole and Bristol at certain times in the 1650s, the actions of the soldiers in removing popular ministers upon suspicion of disloyalty and in patronising gathered churches provoked the townspeople to real hatred. Yet the latter were not powerless to retaliate, because their complaints and demonstrations often embarrassed the central government into gestures of conciliation. At Hull a governor to whom the corporation especially objected was eventually transferred to Scotland, at Poole the commander was replaced with a less controversial individual and at Bristol the garrison was withdrawn altogether. It can hardly be imagined that the army was ever popular in the mid-1650s as it was maintained by heavy taxation and was a very visible reminder that the regime had no faith in the goodwill of its subjects. Yet to say that it was generally detested may, perhaps, be an exaggeration.[10].

This is the context for that most spectacular episode of military rule in the provinces, the work of the Major-Generals. Yet again, it is difficult to evaluate its impact except in terms of

particular regions and individuals. The Major-Generals themselves had little in common except distinguished war records.
They included first-rank politicians like Lambert, Fleetwood
and Disbrowe, with figures who had hitherto enjoyed little
prominence even within the army. They varied in their quantity
of energy, their attitudes to royalists, to religion and to provin-
cials, their social and regional origins, and their notions upon
how best to raise and dispose of the decimation tax. At one
extreme was William Goffe, who controlled Sussex, Hampshire
and Berkshire, and poured out to Thurloe his despair of ever
being able to understand his counties, make any impact upon
them or secure the co-operation of their leaders. His wails might
arouse more sympathy if they had not been uttered upon the
second day of his office. At the other extreme was Charles
Worsley, put in charge of Cheshire, Lancashire and Staffordshire, who appears to have worked, by all criteria, about three
times as hard as any of his colleagues and exhausted himself so
completely that he broke down and died after one year. One of
the very few characteristics which the Major-Generals did share
was that none came from the pre-war ruling elite, for they
ranged in their origins from minor gentry to goldsmiths. Likewise, they tended to promote commoners into local power. The
new militias raised upon the proceeds of the decimation tax were
commanded by army officers under the nominal leadship of a
few JPs. Worsley replaced several county officials with very
obscure men, while Disbrowe made a brewer High Sheriff of
Wiltshire and appointed tradesmen to the Somerset Bench. On
the face of things, one would expect that these men would
achieve very different results and yet would all be relatively
unpopular, as parvenus.

That is more or less what we find. All the Major-Generals had
a huge job upon their hands, as their areas of responsibility were
very wide and to execute them they had to keep on riding round
an average of three or four counties. Fleetwood and Lambert had
to appoint deputies in order to cope with their duties in central
politics as well. The single task of assessing royalists for the
decimation tax was a gigantic one, and the more disheartening
in that, as said before, it almost never produced enough to pay

for the new militias. The trouble was that the Council had set the threshold of the tax too high, so that in Kent, for example, out of 500 royalists only 91 were liable. And Kent was the *best* case, the only county in which the yield supported the new militia. It was typical of the Protectorate's curious scruples that, having imposed an arbitrary tax, it feared to alter it without calling a Parliament for the purpose. Furthermore, Cromwell had an irritating way of exempting individuals who appealed to him. Apart from these features, the achievement of the Major-Generals was a pattern of personal variations. Disbrowe and Worsley gaoled several royalists, and exacted large bonds from many others, but James Berry (who controlled Wales) and Edward Whalley (in charge of the East Midlands) took an average twenty small bonds in each county. Worsley forbade race-meetings, Whalley permitted them. Worsley, Whalley and Berry all believed in the improvement of public morals and shut down alehouses (Worsley closed 200). On the other hand, the only discernible impact of Disbrowe's rule upon Wiltshire consisted of an unsuccessful attempt to stop a Whitsun wake and a successful one to muzzle several large dogs. Goffe seems to have done absolutely nothing except to raise the militia. Disbrowe locked up Quaker leaders, Berry released them. Whalley alone seems to have been worried about the enclosure of common lands, Disbrowe alone about the composition of juries. Even when they achieved something, the success was often impermanent. All the militias, of course, vanished with the tax. And at least some of the alehouses closed by Worsley were back in business once he was dead.

The question of their popularity also admits of no simple answer. None of those whose reports survive encountered any ill-will or obstruction during the time of their rule. They did not usurp the traditional work of civilian local government, which continued alongside their efforts. Indeed, they rarely attended Quarter Sessions or Assizes themselves, and campaigns such as Worsley's against alehouses were carried on with the co-operation of local leaders who wanted their areas cleaned up. Disbrowe, Berry, Whalley and Goffe all made great efforts to work in partnership with the JPs. Essentially they were concerned with security, not administration. Had the Parliament of 1656 been seething with resentment of them, it is hard to see why the MPs took three months to get round to discussing the decimation tax and then only did so when they were propelled into it by Disbrowe. Even then, they denounced the injustice of the tax rather than the actions of the Major-Generals, and during the next two decades the rule of the latter was hardly referred to at all. It was clearly no great trauma for the ruled. On the other hand, if they were not detested then it does not appear that they were wanted. As mentioned above, the Major-Generals and their clients were usurpers within the social as well as the political (and often the religious) order. The comments preserved in the court records of the time as well as in a disparate mass of other evidence illustrate how much the people of mid-seventeenth-century England and Wales disliked being ruled by individuals who were their own social equals or only slightly above them in the hierarchy. Moreover, the debate over the decimation tax in Parliament reveals how firmly many gentry believed that the tax was a foolish reopening of rifts which ought by now to be healing. The verdict of the public upon the whole episode was delivered clearly in the elections to that Parliament. All the Major-Generals succeeded in getting themselves into the House, but everywhere their attempts to bring in their clients (religious or political radicals from the minor gentry or non-landed groups) failed almost totally. This was the more remarkable in view of their control over the timing, location and returning officers of elections. The electorate were (in theory) fairly substantial property-owners, but the total absence of any popular demonstrations in favour of the soldiers' candidates and the occurrence of some furious demonstrations against them indicate that local society as a whole shared in this act of rejection.

A minor aspect of the work of the Major-Generals consisted of the action taken by a few of them to regulate the corporations of some towns. The Council had set up a committee to examine municipal charters, which was potentially quite a serious weapon against the independence of urban government. In 1656 William Boteler, Major-General of the south-east Midlands, purged the corporation of Bedford and ordered the remnant of members to choose people of radical beliefs to fill up the spaces. Hezekiah Haynes, Fleetwood's deputy in East Anglia, re-modelled the corporation of Colchester, and tried to amend the charter of Norwich to confirm the town's domination by members of independent churches. Whalley had an alderman dismissed at Coventry, and Disbrowe obtained the dismissal or resignation of politically suspect members of the councils of Bristol, Tewkesbury and Gloucester. All this added up to a greater interference by central government in town government than had been known for half a decade. But it still did not amount to very much. Even those four commanders named left every other town within their areas alone, and none of their colleagues intervened in municipalities. Lambert's deputy Charles Howard protected four former royalists who had entered the corporation of Carlisle, because he thought them to be good men. The Council ignored Haynes's proposals for the charter of Norwich. And some of the changes which were made proved as transient as most of the Major-Generals' other work: the purged members at Bedford were back as soon as Boteler lost his control of the region. In general, the records of urban government in this period show a studious disinterest in national political affairs, so that there was little reason for the Council or its servants to be roused to great activity in this sphere. The committee for charters remained virtually idle.

It is now time to ask, as was done for the Commonwealth, how effective government was under the Protectorate. On the whole, the same answer may be returned: that considerable results were achieved despite much bickering and some corruption. Most of the all-important assessment was collected very swiftly, so that of £630,000 of it due between June 1657 and December 1658, £571,465 did appear in that time. No matter what the social background or political or religious views of the various JPs happened to be, they performed much the same work as their predecessors over the past century, and just as well. All local branches of the administration had to deal with a central bureaucracy staffed, like themselves, mostly with newcomers who tended to include a higher proportion of radicals under the

Commonwealth than under the Protectorate. Unlike those of the old monarchy, the central civil servants of both the republican regimes held their offices not for life but subject to good performance, and as a result many fewer of them amassed a number of posts solely to maximise income, or were absentee. As the 'reign' of Oliver Cromwell wore on, important advisers of his such as Broghill and Montagu became patronage-brokers within the bureaucracy just as royal favourites had been. On the whole, the government machine had been much expanded by the demands of war and revolution, without being greatly altered in its essential nature, and coped well with the tasks which it was set.

Nonetheless, confusion and misbehaviour remained as noteworthy under the Protectorate as under the Commonwealth. As the pay of the army slid into arrear in the late 1650s, and as that of the navy fell short during the Spanish war, members of the armed forces were given certificates of money owed to them. Some of the officials who issued these soon set up a ready trade in forging them or in buying them back from the recipients at a discount and redeeming them later at face value. Civil servants were careful to conceal their more dubious transactions, but even so some twenty-four cases of embezzlement were discovered among naval officials, while the Pett family's cunning management of the Chatham dockyard made them a fortune. Money continued to stick to the fingers of some provincial collectors, and different county commissions to argue with each other. In Kent, Wales and the North, excise officers became almost a law unto themselves, following their own practices and procedures with such determination that even the Major-Generals could not force them to return to those established by the central government. The Protectorate, like the old monarchy, found difficulty in persuading men to undertake the burdensome duties of High Sheriff, and it increasingly took to reappointing the same individuals. Communications remained faulty, so that in 1656 two former royalists sponsored a horse race in Hampshire, in apparent ignorance of the fact that the central government had just banned such events as security risks. They came to no harm, because the local government was equally ignorant of the ban.

The growth in the size of the governing machinery had not meant any real centralisation of rule: rather, the central regime maintained more agents in the provinces, fitted into local bodies. And even these agents operated in different ways, according to personality and circumstance. The complexity of the Protectorate's strength and weaknesses may be illustrated from one case study, Penruddock's rebellion. The Council had repeatedly warned the militia commissions, JPs and regular soldiers in Hampshire and Wiltshire that a royalist rising was imminent. Yet they were all taken by surprise when Penruddock's band gathered, and all that stopped the royalists from inflicting any damage was the pathetic smallness of their numbers, 400 at their strongest. Once the enemy was in arms, the militia committees went into action, and within two days had 4000 men on foot to attack Penruddock. None were needed, as a horse troop from the regular army did the work unaided. As the militia gathered, they were mocked by some of their fellow villagers, who told them that they would never get paid, and indeed it seems likely that they were not paid in full. From one point of view, these events had been a demonstration of the power and efficiency of the regime. From another, they had been a shambles.

At village level, the rule of the Protectorate would hardly have differed from that of the Commonwealth. With the worst problems resulting from the years of civil war and harvest failure now solved, there was more time for the reformation of manners and morals if local rulers were inclined to take it. As noted, some Major-Generals were ready to lead this work. A number of popular sports and festivities had already been prohibited in the 1640s. The Purged Parliament had extended the terms and penalties of previous acts against the infringement of the Sabbath and they were further elaborated in 1657. At times during the 1650s justices in Sussex, the East Riding, Hampshire and Lancashire made collective orders to enforce and to supplement these regulations. Yet even in those counties, let alone others, no boom in prosecutions followed these gestures, and action against alehouses, merry-making and breaches of the sabbatarian laws remained sporadic and (save for Worsley's campaign) small-scale. Perhaps even many of the Protectorate's

JPs were more interested in security and good neighbourliness than moral reform, and perhaps in many villages there was little that needed reforming. The main novelty in the provinces after 1653 was the effect of the Little Parliament's law instituting civil marriage, which reduced an existing situation of complexity and uncertainty to complete confusion. Before 1640 it had been unclear whether a ceremony of betrothal or a wedding in church represented the true moment of union. Now many people remained equally in doubt upon this issue, while having to cope with the unprecedented experience of being wed by a JP in addition. Officially, the latter form was now the only legal one. In practice, many couples continued to marry in a religious gathering, some in church according to the Anglican Prayer Book or the presbyterian *Directory*, and some in a gathered congregation or Quaker meeting according to such declaration as they chose. Very often this happened as well as the civil ceremony, but sometimes it took place instead of that, and all contemporaries agreed that the idea of marrying before a JP was generally unpopular. Broghil and some others among Cromwell's civilian councillors attacked it in Parliament during 1657. Sometimes ministers got away with conducting weddings, but many were indicted for it. Often parishes drew the local clergyman into the civil process by electing him as the registrar. Others allegedly mocked it by electing the village drunk or fornicator. Some JPs tried to wipe out betrothal ceremonies or to ensure that a couple were fit to wed, while others clearly married people at a glance. The most unfortunate victim of the whole situation was probably the Wiltshire man who was wed before Hampshire justices. When he returned home with his wife, the local magistrates declared the union illegal because it had not taken place before them. He obediently shed his bride, and somehow married another woman. Whereupon the same Wiltshire JPs issued a warrant for his arrest for bigamy. The Little Parliament had furnished the law with an opportunity to make a particularly ill-tempered ass of itself.

If most of the previous few paragraphs have been devoted to the Protectorate's servants and collaborators, who were its inveterate enemies? Who were the diehard royalists who took part in the conspiracies and risings which did occur? They were not the leaders of the King's regiments or civilian commissions during the Great Civil War, who were either dead, in exile or reduced to exhausted passivity. Nor were most of them members of the traditional social elite, however alienated that elite now clearly was. They were a mixture of younger sons of nobility and gentry, lesser gentry, merchants, tradespeople and artisans. When the Major-Generals noted down individuals as especially worthy of suspicion, they regarded people from the middle ranks of society as just as active and dangerous as those from the landowning class. Innkeepers featured prominently, as their occupation provided excellent opportunities to host conferences and to convey information. The conspirators do not seem to have been distinguished in their political and religious attitudes from those royalists who remained passive. What made them into activists was an exceptional zeal for the royalist cause and a personaly taste for an exciting life. They were exemplified by John Mordaunt, one of the most prominent of them both in operations and (as the younger brother of an earl) in his birth. In 1658 he escaped being found guilty and sentenced to death by a single vote in a High Court of justice. He walked out of the courtroom, and commenced a new plot immediately. The presence of a few junior sprigs of the nobility made the active royalists look like a more socially distinguished group than the leaders of the Commonwealth and Protectorate. On the whole, however, both sets were a sample of all ranks of society, with the same relative concentration in the middle layers, and both were an equally unusual group of individuals.

Thus far assembled, this picture of the country under the Protectorate would suggest that although the ruled might not like their rulers much in principle, they had little to worry about in practice,. But the introduction of another element into it must alter such a conclusion completely. It is that same factor which gave such a terrible febrility to the whole early modern period in Western Europe, which roused Scotland and Ireland to rebellion in the late 1630s and early 1640s, which made the English Civil War so bitter and which nerved the army which won that war to bring about the English Revolution: the factor of religion. It is time now to scan the spectrum of faith under the Protectorate as under the Commonwealth, and see what, if anything, had developed in it.

Little had altered in the position of the Roman Catholics. The Council and the Parliament sometimes made savage gestures at them, as the ancestral enemy, but they remained in practice of little concern. The Protectorate continued to levy fines upon them stringently for failing to attend Protestant worship, and yet their financial sufferings were to some extent compensated for, with a novel freedom. The regime had so many pressing worries that as long as the Catholics behaved inoffensively (which they did), they were able to harbour their priests, attend their private masses and travel about the country with more ease than uder the late King for whom so many of them had suffered. By contrast, the attitude of the government to the Protestant episcopalians, until 1642 the leaders of the English Church, became tougher as the 1650s wore on. This was not because of any activity by the deposed bishops, who all lived quietly in retirement and ignored appeals from the exiled court to replace those of their number who died. As they were all relatively old men, it appeared that another decade would bring about the natural extinction of the former Anglican hierarchy. Yet there remained considerable energy among the episcopalians. A former Church of Ireland bishop, settled at Cumberworth in Yorkshire, continued to ordain clergy from all over the North who felt happier accepting livings in the Protectorate's Church if they had episcopal approval as well. The author of *Eikon Basilike*, John Gauden, himself; held a benefice and represented an unknown but probably considerable number who were prepared to serve the new religious order but fervently hoped for a counter-revolution. Some, like John Hackett, vented their feelings by preaching against the new system even while they observed its forms. Yet others, such as Henry Hammond, Gilbert Sheldon and Peter Heylyn, refused to deal with the Interregnum Church at all. Most of them took refuge with royalist gentry, and between them they published a long series of works explaining and defending their beliefs. As chaplains, schoolteachers, tutors and parish lecturers, they were potentially a considerable influence upon a future generation. It was the fear of this that led Cromwell and his Council, as part of their great over-reaction to Penruddock's rebellion, to attempt to drive former royalist clergy out of most of those occupations. For good measure, they ordered their local representatives, including the Major-Generals, to crack down upon use of the pre-war Prayer Book in churches and private services. The effect of this campaign was very limited. A string of prosecutions did result, but use of the Prayer Book continued even in London, and the die-hard episcopalians kept on publishing and corresponding at the same speed. None of this would have been possible without the support of a large number of people from all classes who wanted to have the old style of service, from the old style of churchman.

Still, if the government had only limited success in stamping out the episcopalians, there was some progress in the reconstruction of the national Church which, if completed, might have rendered such conservatives redundant in the eyes of most parishioners. The system of Triers and Ejectors had solved the problem of the provision of clergy, and if there was as yet no national doctrine, then the Protectorate's ecclesiastical policy depended upon the belief that one was best evolved from below rather than imposed from above. Cromwell certainly saw the role of his administration as being to preserve order while Protestants of different opinions debated those differences until they achieved agreement or accepted co-existence within the same national framework. There was still a lot of repairing to be done. In 1654 the Protector and Council set up trustees to continue the Commonwealth's policy of augmenting stipends, but even by the mid-1650s many parishes had no ministers to be assisted. Wales, where proverbial poverty of livings and a language barrier discouraged newcomers, was probably the worst affected region. There 700 benefices were empty and public religion could only be provided by itinerant preachers of the sort established by the Commission for the Propagation of the Gospel. Only two of the national panel of Triers were Welsh. Elsewhere the presbyterian *classes* continued to dissolve. Especially in rural districts of the North, there was a serious problem of decaying church fabric, because parishes were too demoralised or uninterested to maintain it. Bickering continued between sets of parishioners and between parishioners and ministers over the form of religion which took place in their church. The most celebrated case came in 1657, at the parish of St Bartholomew Exchange in London, where Cromwell himself had become the patron. He chose as the new incumbent the pastor of a gathered congregation, who brought his whole flock with him when he occupied the church building. To the Protector, this was a symbol of the sort of reconciliation which he wanted in the nation. To the parishioners, it was the capture of their church by a sect, and they slammed its doors upon these alleged intruders. Cromwell proceded to impose the minister, and his old followers, upon the parish by direct command backed with the threat of force.

To some extent, however, the vision of the Protector and his Council was being fulfilled. In towns such as Newcastle-upon-Tyne and York, the number of able preaching minsters was probably greater than ever before. Furthermore, whole sections of the provinces had become grouped in regional associations of clergy, to provide joint action and a common framework for ordination and discipline. Membership was entirely voluntary, and included both beneficed ministers and clerical pastors of independent churches. They appeared in Worcestershire and in Cumberland and Westmorland at the same moment in 1653, and by the time of Cromwell's death eleven other counties had produced them. They united moderate episcopalians, presbyterians, congregational independents and even a few baptists, so that clerics who had condemned each other's existence during the 1640s were now working together. Most parishes were held by men who expressed no strong doctrinal views. During the course of the Protectorate's existence, at least 130 ministers who were also preachers to gathered congregations accepted places in the national Church. In July 1658 presbyterians holding fellowships at the two universities made a joint announcement of desire for concord with the independent churches. All this would have represented a situation of immense comfort to the ministers concerned, to the government and to many laity if it had been a matter of forgiveness and concilation in a religious world in which contests had been rendered politically impossible. But it was not. It consisted, rather, of a redrawing of battle lines as old enemies found themselves mutually under attack from new and terrifying opponents.

Some of the latter included the still increasing numbers of gathered churches which rejected the concept of a national organisation altogether. In most towns with large garrisons they were planted and fostered by the soldiers, and missionary efforts or spontaneous interest formed more elsewhere. As before, they tended to appear in urban centres or in rural districts with weak gentry control, but this was not always true. Parishes with traditionally strong manorial authority sometimes threw up sectaries, as a result of accident of personalities: the English and Welsh were not automatically programmed in their beliefs by their environment. It is, as before, the baptists who have left us the best records of their progress. By 1660 their churches numbered 250, including between them perhaps 25,000 people. The latter were probably equally divided between the more numerous but smaller Particular Baptist congregations and the fewer but larger General Baptist meetings. Not only were there now more of them but they were better organised. The Particular Baptists had by 1658 formed four regional associations, covering large areas such as the West Country and Midlands. Although there was no national meeting, London pastors exercised a paramount influence over the whole movement. The General Baptists were more fluidly structured, but they did have a regular meeting of delegates in the capital. This sort of development did not have to worry people of more conservative beliefs. The sects remained divided from each other by a range of doctrinal squabbles, and even the baptists had important differences. Some of the latter made common cause with the official churchmen of Northumberland to destroy a rival baptist group at Hexham. A few baptist ministers, as described, co-operated with parish clergy. Greater organisation meant a better supervision of members, and the control of possible individual excesses or very extreme views. The Fifth Monarchists had been crippled by the arrest of so many of their leaders, culminating in 1657 when Thurloe's agents reported a plan by one of their churches for an armed rising in London. The entire group was arrested just as it was preparing to hoist a banner of the Lion of Judah, and placed (without trial) in indefinite detention. The sects had always disdained the populace as a whole and placed their hopes in the army and government. After 1654 it was clear that the Protectorate was not going to listen to their demands, and that left them to wait upon events. What made them continue to seem menacing to many in the population was that their programme had been adopted by a much more dynamic and effective group. For 1654 was also the year in which the Quakers came south.

Within four years they had penetrated every county, and indeed most parishes, within England and Wales. Their greatest number of conversions were made to the counties north and east of London, in Somerset and Wiltshire and in Warwickshire and Worcestershire. In 1657 London itself took over from the North as their greatest stronghold, probably followed by Bristol. As before, they tended to spread through networks of existing separatist religious groups and then to work outwards into the public at large. Some commoners in southern England had already, by 1651, rejected the paramountcy of Scripture in favour of personal revelation (as described earlier), so that the Quaker teachings often fell amongst an audience prepared to receive them. Their preachers were soon drawing crowds numbering thousands. The total of actual converts was still relatively tiny, but it expanded far more swiftly than that of any other radical religious group. In 1652 there had been about 500, in 1654 about 5000, and in 1657 there were perhaps 20,000. By 1660 there might have been anything from 30,000 to 60,000. Even the higher figure comprised only just over 1 per cent of the total population, but had such a rate of growth been maintained then all England and Wales would, in theory, have become Quaker in one generation. No wonder their evangelists worked with such high morale and apocalyptic vision. At the time that Naylor was brought before Parliament in December 1656, many of the MPs had never set eyes on a Quaker but all had heard of them. They had replaced Levellers, Diggers and Ranters as the new Menace To Society.

Their strength was in those social ranks which had always supplied most religious radicals, and given them their own membership in the North. They attracted the benevolent interest of a few minor gentry and clerics, but in general they had even less appeal to these groups than had the baptists. The army officers who protected so many gathered congregations were palpably more dubious about the Quakers. There were conversions among the rank and file of the soldiers, and a few of their leaders were sympathetic. But the Portsmouth garrison arrested a preacher and the companies guarding the Isle of Wight prevented any from landing there. The overwhelming majority of early Quakers were yeomen, husbandmen, wholesalers, artisans or retailers, and what distinguished them socially from the various independent churches was the very great appeal which they had to rural people. Most of their male leaders were younger sons, and women continued to supply almost half their evangelists. From the beginning, their founders had been careful to co-ordinate action and to correspond regularly, and in 1657 they instituted general meetings to prevent a loss of coherence resulting from so swift an expansion. Yet it does seem that the historian has to reckon with a different type of 'Quaker' from those who attended such meetings, whose activities are meticulously recorded in the documents preserved in Friends House Library, and who grew into the later Society of Friends. This is the person who was quite happy to absorb the doctrine of personal revelation and the redundancy of a visible Church, while wishing to remain outside the main Quaker movement and rejecting its moral solemnity. They would have overlapped with or sprung from those local sceptics and scoffers who appear with some regularity before the pre-war church courts. Such people feature in the observations of individuals hostile to all religious radicals, especially in 1659 as 'Quakers'. To the Quakers 'proper', and some baptists, they were 'Ranters', a borrowing of the great smear-term of the early 1650s. In this manner a number of semantic traps were unwittingly prepared for the future historian.[11]

Not that the Quakers 'proper' were any less shocking to all other religious groups and to most of the population. The twin pillars of their faith, the rejection of any visible Church and of the primacy of Scripture, made them almost as appalling to baptists as to presbyterians or episcopalians. By implication their religious beliefs struck at the notion of a social hierarchy, and some of their other tenets did so directly. They denounced all distinctions of dress as worldly vanities, refused to remove their hats to any being except God, and addressed all individuals as 'thee', holding that this form was grammatically correct and ignoring the fact that it was generally used only upon inferiors. They certainly condemned profanity, strong drink, sports, merry-making and sexual misdemeanours, but the flamboyant tactics of evangelism which they had evolved in the North seemed to many to be equally morally questionable. After 1654 no community knew when a Quaker missionary, often naked, might not appear in the market place to denounce the sins of the community or might not interrupt the church service to revile the minister. Their printed words were often just as intemperate, and by 1658 they had published over 500 tracts. Instead of lobbying the government they went straight to the people: by changing humans they intended to change the political system, reversing the attitude of the Levellers and Fifth Monarchists. Yet their political programme (though varied and incoherent) still reproduced many of the demands of those groups, for codification of the law, for the abolition of lawyers and of universities, for a limit to the accumulation of wealth and for annual Parliaments. Upon the question of the legitimacy of armed force, they had as yet delivered no judgement, as peaceful evangelism seemed to be achieving such good results. Their greatest efforts to secure reform, understandably, were directed against tithes, and characteristically they consisted not merely of a campaign for their legal abolition but also of a simple refusal to pay them.

Of the Major-Generals, Fleetwood, Lambert, Berry and Worsley showed the same relative clemency towards Quakers as Cromwell himself, but Haynes, Goffe and Disbrowe were hostile to them and Boteler an active persecutor. Unsurprisingly, Boteler's attitude was shared, and intensified, by most of the social elite. From 1656 onward, justices and corporations across most of the country made efforts to halt them, employing the laws against the disturbing of the peace and of church services, blasphemy, vagrancy, contempt of court and non-payment of tithes, and refusal of the oaths used for the detection of Catholics (which Quakers could not take as they believed all oaths to be profane). Devout gentry and magistrates saw them as a danger to people's souls as well as to public order, and some sincerely believed them to be agents sent by Jesuits to undermine the Protestant Church. By mid-1659 over 2000 Quakers had been committed to prison. But this hostility on the part of the elite was underpinned by a considerable amount of animosity upon the part of commoners. Mobbing, rather than arrest, was the principal danger faced by evangelists. Ordinary people often detested Quakers as busybodies, killjoys, nuisances, republicans, reputed witches and (above all) as outsiders, commonly with northern accents. Local louts were able to have a great deal of brutish fun with them, encouraged by the very magistrates and constables who normally prevented such horseplay. Pamphlets and seminars impressed upon the public the horror which the Quakers represented. As before, the Quaker movement appealed to a particular type of personality, which was always going to be in a minority. But that did not make it any less frightful to many in the majority, especially as, over the past ten years, minority beliefs had consistently taken over the national government. The Protectorate seemed to be resistant to those of the Quakers, but it was a much more passive resistance than many people wanted. Whatever the feelings of some of its members, the Council obstinately refused to let Quakers be punished for what they said, as opposed to some of the things that they did. By 1658 a lot of the English and Welsh were seriously worried about the situation. Cromwell died leaving a government which was potentially politically and financially bankrupt, and provinces which were the scene of more division and anxiety than they had been at the beginning of his Protectorate.

III   British and European Affairs

After the amazing military achievements of the Commonwealth

outside England and Wales, the work of the Protectorate abroad ought to have been more modest and less onerous, consolidating English rule over Ireland and Scotland and making peace with the Dutch. Matters turned out rather differently. The manner in which the other British realms were settled acquired graver implications for the English than would have been expected in 1653, a fresh war had to be fought in Scotland, and a new conflict was begun with a Continental power which was to be at once more glorious and more damaging than that with the Dutch.

In Ireland the Protectorate displayed as little interest in the Catholic majority as the Commonwealth had done. By 1657 priests were returning to the country in large numbers, amazed that so little was done to stop them or to convert their flocks. Most of the efforts of the new government and the controversies which resulted were focused upon the new Protestant elite, and upon the practical needs of the administration. The dominant figure from 1652 until 1655 was Fleetwood, as Lord Deputy, who was prepared to support a large-scale programme of installing preachers and opening schools, using radicals from England as his agents. Instead, all the money at the disposal of the government was needed to keep up the army of occupation, so that the reform programme was virtually stillborn. All that resulted was a rapid growth of gathered churches within the army, founded by the officers whom Fleetwood employed as his trusted subordinates. The baptists became particularly powerful, so that by 1654 they were thought by many to have a stranglehold upon the system of promotion. But in that year Fleetwood's system began to crumble, because Cromwell sent out his younger son Henry to command the army in Ireland. This individual rapidly became the guiding personality in the land. Fleetwood, feeling undermined, left it in disgust the next year and in 1657 Henry obtained the title of Lord Deputy for himself.

Ireland's new master was twenty-six years old when he landed at Dublin, and therefore, like Thurloe and some of his father's other civilian councillors, had never fought in the English Civil War. The fervour which had produced the English Revolution was quite unknown to him, and he had no feeling either for reform or for charismatic religion. Instead, he sought stable government based upon a reconciliation of all parties. As a result, as soon as he arrived he ended the supremacy of the baptists in his army. Because they would not accept a position of mere parity with other groups, they instantly became his determined enemies, forcing him to turn to more conservative individuals who were in any case more companionable to his temperament. At first he found them among those of his council in Dublin who believed in independent churches but also in the continued co-existence of a national body. Soon, however, he was becoming even more closely associated with the pre-war ('old') Protestant settlers of the island, the most politically active of whom, Lord Broghil, was already such a favourite of his father's. Most of these people, had, like Broghil, been royalists, but they received very different treatment from those in England. The 'Old Protestants' of Munster were pardoned *en masse* by the Protector and Council in 1654, because so many of them had defected to Cromwell soon after his initial victories. The others were theoretically liable to heavy fines, but Henry Cromwell studiously neglected to collect these. From 1656 he set about the work of re-establishing the Church of Ireland. Henceforth he showed open hostility to all sectaries and halted Quaker penetration of the country by arresting their missionaries and dismissing or browbeating any army officers who showed an interest in their message. Since the conquest, the state Church had consisted of a set of ministers paid from a fund provided by the lands of the defunct bishops, deans and chapters. It was clear that this money was insufficient to pay for very many, and that more had to be found. To the young Cromwell the obvious solution was to restore tithes, a decision which not only drew upon him the unwavering hatred of the sects but alienated those 'congregational independents' who had accepted the state Church. His main ecclesiastical adviser was now a former dean of the old Church, Edward Worth, who had founded an association of ministers in Munster similar to those in England, save for the significant difference that it was closed to all pastors of gathered congregations. The pre-war Scottish settlers in Ulster, who had set up a presbyterian system like their native Kirk, were encouraged by

Henry to extend and to consolidate this. In 1658 these two groups dominated an assembly of churchmen in Dublin, which formally reimposed tithes upon the nation. Parallel to this process took place the restoration of old-fashioned secular government. In 1655 experiments in Munster, of putting judges upon salaries instead of letting them take fees, and streamlining of legal procedures, were halted as too controversial. At the same time Justices of the Peace were recommissioned all over the island, mixing 'Old Protestants' with present and former soldiers and new settlers, all chosen for their loyalty to the regime. Henry Cromwell tried, with some success, to make sure that they were also personally loyal to himself. By 1658 he firmly believed that he had stabilised the country and established his father's government securely there, by taking the pre-war Protestant ruling elite into partnership irrespective of its previous political record. In the process he had jettisoned the sort of people who had made the English Revolution, and scrapped their ideas as well. What was particularly significant was that he made it plain to everybody that he wished the same policy to be employed to settle England.

It was also significant that during the same period Henry Cromwell himself believed that he had a legitimate cause for grievance, and that the source of this lay in the government at Westminster. In part this was due to the usual negligence, carelessness and stupidity with which most English administrations undertook their share of ruling Ireland. Although all legislative power had now been transferred to the Parliament at Westminster, executive power was divided ill-definedly between the Protector and Council and the Lord Deputy and his council, the former in theory being responsible for major decisions of policy. Repeatedly, Henry sent his father requests for advice or action, and repeatedly followed them with irritable reminders, because no replies had been received. The most glaring example of this came in 1657, when Ireland technically had no government at all for two months, because Fleetwood's commission as Lord Deputy had expired but Henry's had not been sent to replace it. Like monarchs before and after him, Oliver Cromwell gave the administration in Dublin palpitations by making grants of land in Ireland to followers in England, without any notion of the damage which the subtraction of these rents would do to the Irish public revenue. Protector and Council also ignored several appeals to do something about the debased state of the nation's currency or to divert warships to chase away pirates who were hunting along the coasts. On the other hand, Henry's administration could sometimes use its distance from Westminster for its own ends, just like other Dublin-based governments before and after. In 1657 the Second Protectorate Parliament decided upon the grandiloquent gesture of imposing an oath abjuring the Pope upon all Irish Catholics. Both the Lord Deputy and the 'Old Protestants' protested vehemently that this was a pointlessly provocative scheme, and when they were ignored, they simply neglected to enact it properly.

The young Cromwell was still more annoyed by political problems, arising directly from his father's failings as a statesman. Oliver liked, as said above, to have followers of opposed opinions and principles, balanced against each other. This would have been perhaps a wise tactic if they had represented powerful interests in the nation, but as it was he was creating divisions and rivalries in an already small and embattled ruling circle. At least in England it had the effect of enlarging the sources of advice given to him, but in Ireland the same tactic could hardly have had even that benefit. His original action in taking the army away from Fleetwood's direct command and giving it to his own not very experienced son could only have been to strengthen his own influence in the land and to balance two clients against each other. He may also have wished to check the radicals, whom his son-in-law favoured, with the views of Henry, who had been a prominent 'moderate' in the Little Parliament. Yet having allowed his son to supplant Fleetwood, he gave him no support in his efforts to settle Ireland in a different fashion. Henry carried them out anyway, enraged not only by the lack of response to his appeals to the English government, but also by the fact that he had no control over the membership of the council which was supposed to advise him in Dublin. Oliver had ultimate responsibility for that, and saw to it that all the enemies whom Henry's policies had made remained upon it, unable to do more than hamper the Lord Deputy and create a greater bitterness between him and them. Even more than in England, the example of Ireland reveals the Lord Protector's talent for ensuring that none of his followers could blame him personally for anything, while they all became steadily more at odds with each other. This was the more worrying in that the government in London had also landed Henry with a very serious problem which threatened to undermine his authority. The Commonwealth had paid for its rule over Ireland by imposing an assessment of £30,000 per month upon the country and shipping over an average £22,000 per month in addition. As part of its general policy of reducing assessments and armies, the Protectorate brought the Irish tax down to £10,000 per month in 1654. Just as in England, the soldiers were not disbanded to a number that the new level of taxation could pay, so that a deficit appeared. Just as in England, also, the Second Protectorate Parliament made the situation worse. It reduced the Irish assessment to £9000 per month, and the financial difficulties of the English government meant that henceforth no more than £8000 per month could be sent to Dublin. Yet nobody thought that any further disbanding of the army of occupation would be safe. The result was that, as in England, the gap in the public revenue became serious. During 1658 it amounted to £96,000, and the army's pay fell nine months into arrear. And a badly-paid army was always a worry to its commander. In both realms the Protectorate had achieved a level of taxation which the public felt to be too high and yet which provided far less than the state needed.

So, if the Cromwellian regime created both successes and difficulties in Ireland what did it achieve for the land itself? One reply would be that it confirmed the Commonwealth's establishment of the Protestant Ascendancy. Under the Protectorate the massive transfer of land ordered by the Purged Parliament was carried out and Protestants were commissioned as JPs and constituted as urban councils over the island. It was under the same regime that other steps (or the failure to take some) ensured that those Protestants would remain a minority. The lack of any drive to convert the Catholics has been noted. It was accompanied by an equal inability to attract over large numbers of English to swamp them. The Commonwealth had expected to settle more than 35,000 soldiers, and 1000 people to whom the state owed money. At the end of the next decade, when a survey of the result was taken, 7500 of the former and 500 of the latter were actually present. Nor had English tenants and traders arrived as expected, and in default of them the new landlords and municipalities were anxious to retain the local Catholics instead of deporting them as the Purged Parliament had wished. The only contribution made by the Protectorate to the welfare of the whole land was to abolish some duties on imports, to permit farmers to restock their lands. By 1658 the total volume of Irish trade was back to 80 per cent of that recorded in 1638, despite the hideous destruction of the 1640s. But the English government was also determined, as before and after, to stunt Irish exports to prevent them from competing with English products. Political union did not include any compensating economic benefits. By no stretch of argument could the English conquest of 1649–53 be said to have been 'good' for Ireland.

In Scotland the Protectorate initially did not merely have the task of settling the country, but also that of preventing it from slipping out of English hands once again. As has been said, Cromwell and Monck effectively conquered the Lowlands, and then accepted the formal submission of the Highland chiefs, who no longer had a royal government to obey. This situation left most of the clans behind the Highland Line with their fighting strength and stocks of weaponry intact. It was liable to explode as soon as one of two developments occurred. The first was that the English began trying to interfere seriously with the Highlanders. The second was that an exiled royalist government reconstituted itself, to legitimise Scottish resistance. Both happened in the course of 1652. In late 1651 the Purged Parliament had appointed a commission of eight important soldiers and politicians to manage Scotland, headed by Lambert and Monck. It had also imposed an assessment, of £13,500 per month, two and a half times as heavy as any tax previously laid upon the country, and prepared to unite the two nations formally. During 1652 it restored the municipalities, and appointed a Supreme Court (mostly Englishmen) and High Sheriffs (half of whom were English army officers). Officials were only installed if they swore loyalty to the Commonwealth, and municipalities only allowed to function if they accepted the union with England. A wholly English commission was established to approve all appointments to the national Kirk. During the summer two English columns paraded through the Highlands in an attempt to overawe the chiefs and to receive the submissions of those few who had sent none. Having done all this, the Commonwealth considered that the settlement of the nation was well under way, and reduced both the assessment and the occupying army by over a fifth. To supervise the country, it appointed a capable if rather querulous soldier, Robert Lilburne, and then more or less turned its back upon it to concentrate upon the Dutch war. At that point the explosion occurred.

The Commonwealth's mistake had been to humiliate the Highlanders and then to run down its army. Before the end of the year a group of chiefs led by Angus Macdonald of Glengarry had contacted Charles II to ask for commissions to rise in his name. The exiled royalists showed a skill which was to be missing from their dealings with English conspirators, in encouraging, reconciling and co-ordinating the different activists. More and more chieftains joined, and a respected Lowland nobleman, the Earl of Glencairn, became the formal leader of the rebellion. As soon as the snows melted in 1653, they went into action, striking from the mountains in small parties and evading all attempts by the English forces to contain them or to bring them to battle. Lilburne responded with as much energy as the limitations of his genius and of his resources allowed. He granted reductions in the assessment of those chiefs who collaborated with him, and tried to make an alliance with those Scots who had been most reluctant to work with Charles II. He also harassed ministers who still prayed for the King and made landowners, parish officers and JPs responsible for stopping the people in their jurisdictions from joining the rebels. All these efforts probably succeeded in making the rebellion slightly less serious than it actually became, but that was quite serious enough. Lilburne proved unable to stop the royalists, who were employing tactics and a terrain which had defeated every invader since the Romans. By early 1654, their bands were roving across the entire country as far as the Border, and Charles II had sent a relatively capable and respected soldier, John Middleton, to draw them together.

In reality, Middleton's task was impossible and it is unlikely that the rebels could ever have done more than to maintain an indefinite guerilla war in the mountain and hill areas. They never possessed the manpower and equipment to take on the Commonwealth's soldiers in a straight fight, and they could not co-operate with each other for long. Ruinous quarrels kept breaking out between their leaders, while similar personal rivalries, plus some shrewd calculation, meant that the majority of Highland chiefs (let alone Lowland magnates) remained neutral or helped the English. But then, this decentralised and chaotic nature of the rebellion was the very thing which made it so hard to deal with. An exceptional general and a proportionate military effort were required from the newly-instituted Protectorate, and they were provided. In April 1654 Cromwell sent George Monck back to command in Scotland, with about 3000 more men and £50,000 to pay them. Monck's tactics were to send his soldiers into the Highlands in separate columns, with sufficient supplies to permit them to keep moving swiftly through the passes, unhampered by any need to return to bases to revictual. Each soldier had a week's bread in his knapsack, while packhorses carried more bread and some cheese alongside them. In this fashion they covered almost a thousand miles in three months, burning the crops and killing the cattle of the royalists and trying to catch them. Exhausted and starving, the rebels began swiftly to despair. Monck was all for putting their leaders to death, but the Protector and Council wisely coupled political clemency with his military ruthlessness and promised a complete pardon to all who submitted. A few diehards held out through the winter, but in May 1655 the last came in and Middleton fled back abroad to his royal master.

As the campaign progressed, all the reforming energy of the early Protectorate was bent towards completing the settlement of the country. Ordinances formally united it to England, gave relief to debtors and improved the provision of justice. From the beginning a role in government was given to some Scots, by the decision to permit Highland chiefs and Border lairds to police their own areas: the futility of trying to disarm the hill and mountain people and to rule them directly was recognised. Over half the MPs returned from Scotland to the First Protectorate Parliament were Scots, and the royalists were treated almost as leniently as those in Ireland, their fines usually being collected only in part or not at all. In May 1655, as the war ended, the Protector and Council transferred executive power from Monck himself to a Council for Scotland, mixing army officers, English officials and Scots. It was instructed to settle the finances of the country and also the Kirk, and was chaired by that ubiquitous Anglo-Irishman, Lord Broghil. It imposed an Excise, got the assessment collected more efficiently, and stabilised the public revenue at £8500 per month. The return of local power to the Scots was continued with the appointment of many gentry as JPs, although as in England most of the nobility and greatest lairds had to be excluded because of their hostility. Only attempts to introduce a system of Triers for the Kirk failed, not because of hostility to the government but because of the divisions between different groups of Scottish churchmen. In the end the appointment of ministers was left to the Council for Scotland. During the last two years of Cromwell's life, Scotland was a peaceful if resentful land. Broghil and most of the Council returned to England, leaving Monck once again the leading figure. He had no trouble with the Scots, his only problems being similar to those of Henry Cromwell, resulting from slow attention to his request by the government in England, the appearance of Quaker missionaries (whom Monck deported) and reduction of the assessment by the Second Protectorate Parliament to a level which could not quite support the army. But the deficit on the public revenue was smaller than that in England or Ireland and by 1658 the administration in Scotland was in many ways the best off of all those in the three British realms.

The Commonwealth had left nothing more in the British archipelago for the Protectorate to conquer: instead, Cromwell's regime extended English territory overseas. He began his tenure of the Protectorship not with an act of war but one of peace, by coming to terms with the Dutch. The struggle with them was clearly reaching the point of exhaustion, and had never been popular with the army officers. Perhaps this was because they were uneasy about a war against a Protestant neighbour, and perhaps they disliked a struggle which turned the limelight away from them onto the navy. Whichever reason was paramount within each individual, the clear result of their attitude was the Treaty of London, signed in April 1654. It was, on paper, a remarkable triumph for the English. They obtained the island of Pula Run in the centre of the East Indies, the area providing the spices which represented Asia's most valuable commodity. Compensation was granted for injuries done to English merchants in that region and in the Baltic, while none was offered for the mass seizures of Dutch shipping. The United Provinces promised to salute English warships, to refuse any help to Charles II and to exclude from power the Dutch House of Orange which had formerly given him assistance. It was all a little less impressive in practice. Pula Run was never actually delivered, the terms of the salute remained ill-defined, and the Dutch government was already determined to have no dealings with Charles and to render the Orangists politically impotent. But as a way out of a deadlocked conflict it saved face handsomely and further boosted English prestige abroad. Six days later a commercial treaty was signed with Sweden. There followed another with Portugal in July and a third with Denmark in September. The Navigation Act continued to be enforced with great ruthlessness, and in 1655 sixty Dutch ships were seized for contravention of it, this time with the glum acquiescence of their government. This group of measures ought to have made the Protectorate a time of increasing prosperity for English foreign trade.

In fact, it was the reverse, and this was entirely the fault of the government. Within four months of the Treaty of London, the Protector and council had decided to launch an utterly unprovoked attack upon Spain, the strongest power in Europe, the best remaining market for English goods and the controller of the most efficient privateer fleet in the world. Any historian who wishes to believe that this decision was the result of noble vision and shrewd calculation needs to come to terms with some notes of the meetings concerned, taken for the benefit of the absent Montagu.[12] A mere fifteen days after the Anglo-Dutch treaty, the Council met to discuss what to do with the 160 warships left in pay at the end of the conflict. It was agreed to turn them against a Catholic power, and of the two greatest, France and Spain, the latter was less tolerant to Protestants and more vulnerable as its territories were much more extensive. Some adventurous sea captains were produced who insisted that the island of Hispaniola in the West Indies would be an easy prize. When somebody objected that the loss of trade with Spain would be enormous, the Council decided that the Spanish would be happy to confine the war to the West Indies and to go on trading with England in European waters. On 20 July it reconsidered the question, Lambert pointing out that the proposed expedition was likely to be difficult and that in the current state of its finances the Protectorate could not afford it. Cromwell himself countered, by saying that God would favour so worthy a cause and that a war would only cost as much as paying off the warships not needed in peacetime. With this incredible suggestion, the resolution to fight appears to have been taken. Had all English foreign policy been conducted with comparable foresight and common sense, then England would probably not now exist.

The expedition against Hispaniola sailed in December 1654. So confident or careless was the government that it put into the preparations none of the care which had been devoted to all the republic's campaigns in the British Isles since 1649. The training, equipment and victuals of the force were all deficient, and it faced a hard-bitten bunch of Spanish colonists who were used to tackling pirates and privateers. The English were driven back to their ships and, for lack of anything better, seized the nearby island of Jamaica instead. This was much more weakly held by the Spanish, for the good reason that it was a much less desirable property: in 1655 its most noteworthy product was mosquitoes. It would take decades to develop, and the Spaniards soon gave notice that they would make a sustained effort to expel the English from it. Meanwhile, the Protectorate was behaving like the bully of Europe. France was locked in a war with Spain which was now two decades old, and Cromwell's government apparently believed that it could rob both with impunity. In 1654 the colonists in New England took neighbouring Acadia from the French, and the Protector and Council refused to give it back. Instead they sent Admiral Robert Blake into the Mediterranean in 1655 to plunder French merchantmen, punish Berber pirates and make a commercial treaty with Tuscany. They were indulging in a game of international smash and grab rather like the regimes controlling Germany and Italy during the late 1930s, and like those regimes they pressed their luck too far. In September 1655 they heard of the humiliation at Hispaniola and of the expensive acquisition of Jamaica. This news was followed by more, that the King of Spain had banned trade with England and unleashed his privateers upon English shipping. Within a few months the Protectorate's customs receipts had suffered a catastrophic fall. Meanwhile Charles II took up residence in Belgium, as the guest of a Spanish government now willing to invade England in concert with a royalist rebellion.

For Cromwell and the Council, apology and the restitution of Jamaica were politically impossible. They pumped money, conscripted soldiers and convict settlers into Jamaica and declared full-scale war against Spain. The trouble was that the Spanish wouldn't offer a fight. Their nimble warships ran rings around the English navy, capturing merchantmen and then making off home. The Council considered a range of attacks upon Spanish territory, such as the capture of Sicily or Cadiz,[13] but eventually settled for trying to intercept the treasure fleets sailing to Andalucia from the Spanish American empire. As Blake's sailors had not been paid for their 1655 expedition, they had to be hunted down and captured to get them back aboard the ships in 1656, a lengthy process. In September of that year some of them (and England) did strike lucky by capturing vessels loaded with silver. The morale of the fleet was raised because the crews concerned got a legal share of the loot (and embezzled more) but the proceeds were nothing like sufficient to solve the government's financial problem. Further progress was only made possible by two developments. One was the decision of the Protector and Council, in November, to accede to a request of the French to send them a brigade of soldiers to help their fight against the Spanish on land. The other was the Second Protectorate Parliament's grant of £400,000. To a government with an already inadequate regular income, fighting a war which cost about £1 million per year, this was not exactly generous. But it combined with extended credit to get the fleet out again.

The results, in 1657, were deeply frustrating. In April the dying Blake accomplished his last great victory, one of the finest in English naval history. Off the Canaries he found and sank an entire treasure fleet, upon which the Spanish had depended to pay their armies. The treasure, however, was ashore in fortresses, from which it could not now be shipped to Spain but which could not be reached by Blake. The beneficiaries were Portugal, which might otherwise have been conquered by a Spanish army that year, and France, which could now at last make some headway in its own long conflict with Spain. The French accordingly used their English brigade to capture two towns in the Netherlands for themselves and one small fort which they handed over to the English. Still, Spain was now crippled, and the next year the Anglo-French force reduced most of West Flanders. Of the towns that fell to it, the French kept five and gave the English one, the port of Dunkirk. The news of this was the only event in the closing months of Cromwell's life which gave him any pleasure.

What, then, was the sum of the Protectorate's achievement abroad? In theory it was spectacular. It had secured England an island in the centre of the East Indies, another in the centre of the West Indies, and the first continental European town which the English had owned for a hundred years. Yet none of these conquests were unqualified assets. Jamaica consumed much more than it yielded for many years, while Pula Run never yielded anything more than the title deeds. Dunkirk had a poor harbour and was badly sited for trade, so that its own utility to the Protectorate was as a sally-port into Europe for expeditions which it could not afford. In fact, it was by no means obvious that the Protectorate could afford Dunkirk. The town would cost £70,000 per year to maintain, adding to the deficit of a public revenue which by the time of Cromwell's death was about £2 million in debt. Perhaps half of this debt had been caused by the war with Spain, and that war was not yet over. After their losses in 1658 the Spanish were ready to agree to France's terms, but not to write off their losses to England. The French accordingly prepared to jettison their English allies and to make peace, leaving the Spanish privateers to continue their inroads into English shipping. The reactions of the public were realistic throughout: none of the Protectorate's victories made it really popular with its subjects, even for a time.

Before leaving this survey of foreign policy between 1653 and 1658, one further set of questions ought to be asked of it. How much was it really a matter of the interests of governments? Were there no economic pressure groups working upon the Council? Did merchants play a part in the formation of its decisions? The answer to all seems to be negative. Of the great trading companies, the Levant, the East India and the Eastland Companies all wanted the Navigation Act, while the Merchant Adventurers and the traders with the English colonies opposed the passage of it. What led the Purged Parliament to choose between their views was not the relative influence of these bodies in politics, but the attitude of its own members towards the Dutch. The only commercial interest which might theoretically have gained from the Spanish war consisted of the traders with Spain, for whom the Protectorate was seeking further opportunities and privileges. But they, apparently uniformly, opposed the conflict. The only 'private interest' to wield some influence was the handful of rather disreputable adventurers who told the Council what most of it already wanted to hear, about the ease of an attack upon the Spanish West Indies. Nor did the Commonwealth or the Protectorate do anything to alter the terms of either domestic or overseas commerce. The Levellers and some of the other radical groups had agitated for the abolition of monopolistic companies in both spheres. Nothing was done, and the rules regulating apprenticeship, guilds, chartered companies and the fixing of wages remained what they had been under the early Stuarts. There was no 'Puritan Revolution' in economics, any more than in morality.

There still remains a need to recount the Protectorate's dealings with a group who could be described, at the time, neither as British, domestic nor part of a foreign power: the Jews. In the thirteenth century they had been expelled from England and never invited to return, although by the 1650s there was a small colony of Sephardic traders living quietly in London. Cromwell was known by 1654 to be favourably disposed towards them himself, but the turning point in his position was the war with Spain. As soon as it broke out, Antonio Fernandez Carvajal, the leader of the London Sephardim, offered the services of his community to the Protector for espionage, employing their strong commercial connections with Spain. A rabbi publicly asked Cromwell for the legal readmission of adherents to the Jewish religion and he referred the matter in turn to a meeting of the whole Council, enlarged by clergymen, merchants and judges. They proved to be so deeply divided over it that the Protector withdrew the question for his own further consideration. In fact, the judges had already supplied him with the answer that he needed, by stating that the medieval expulsion had no enduring validity in common or statute law. So, with a true heroism and magnanimity of vision, he told the Jewish community that they had a legal right to be in England and that he would protect them from prosecution for failing to attend a Christian church service. With his usual political deviousness, he then refused to put this in writing when they asked him to do so. But nobody thereafter questioned the legality of his statement (though some writers vilified him) and the history of modern English Jewry may formally be dated from that moment in 1655. Cromwell's conquest of Jamaica ultimately became one of the most important contributions to that Afro-Caribbean culture which has come to be such a dynamic part of modern English life. His response to the Jews established another cultural tradition, of giving asylum even to strangers who might be ideologically unpalatable to some of the existing population. For that, more than anything else he did, he perhaps deserves to be honoured now.

3

FROM PROTECTORATE TO MONARCHY

It will be obvious enough from the previous chapters that Richard Cromwell inherited an utterly appalling task. He faced it with less experience than any English head of state before or since, as his father's political manoeuvres had denied him either a political or a military command. Instead he had been told to become a quiet Hampshire gentleman, and so he did until being dragged into the limelight shortly before his father's death. In Hampshire his companions had been presbyterian squires, the sort of people who had no feeling of identification with the passions of the soldiers who had produced the English Revolution. He seemed the ideal leader to bring about in England the development which had already taken place in Ireland, the stabilisation of politics by a partnership between the Protectorate and the Protestant gentry, with the independent churches relegated to impotence. That very many conservatively-minded landowners were ready for such a development is indicated by the utter lack of response to Charles II's calls for a rising from even those few who had previously been willing to talk of one. The change of Protector had undoubtedly enhanced the regime's standing in the country. On the other hand, it greatly weakened it in the eyes of that group which had established the regime, the English army. The soldiers had already been worried about the *Humble Petition and Advice*. Their officer corps had changed greatly since 1649 in terms of personnel: over half had been commissioned since then. But their views had, as would become obvious, altered not at all. A majority of them were still apparently either sectaries or members of independent churches, and the junior officers were still more radical than the colonels. At once they began to murmur against Richard as an unknown civilian and after a month they demanded that he resign control over the army. The two most important men in that army were now Fleetwood, who was generally compliant with what the soldiers wished, and Disbrowe, who openly disliked the new Protector. Therefore neither was disposed to crush the agitation. Exactly as in 1648–9, the political concerns of the army were sharpened by material grievances. Their pay slid further and further into arrear, and was losing its value because the harvests had turned bad again, so that by early 1659 the price of bread was almost back to the record level reached ten years before.

Richard Cromwell reacted to this predicament with an admirable courage and strength. He met the officers in person and talked them over just as his father had done seven months before, making Fleetwood the immediate commander but retaining the supreme power and issuing all commissions himself. He raised levels of pay as the Purged Parliament had done. This behaviour secured for him the personal loyalty of certain senior officers such as the former Major-Generals Whalley and Goffe. At the same time he cultivated the friendship of more predictable supporters such as Thurloe and George Monck, who still commanded in Scotland. He also made his brother Lord Lieutenant of Ireland, with full powers over the army there. But none of these achievements could mean much unless he could halt the government's slide into bankruptcy and get the soldiers in all three countries properly paid. The only way to do this, in the view of most of the Council, was to call a Parliament and to try, once more, to get it to co-operate with the Protectorate. This was done as soon as the army had calmed down, and it convened on 27 January 1659.

Presumably as a gesture to please conservative opinion, the Protector and Council had scrapped the electoral reforms of the *Instrument of Government* and returned to the old system whereby boroughs supplied the majority of members. As the Scottish and Irish representatives were still summoned, the result was not only another Cromwellian hybrid but the largest House of Commons yet known, numbering 549. It consisted, on the whole, of the sort of 'conservative' or 'moderate' gentry who had made up the previous two Parliaments, with the distinction that fewer than usual (about a third) had any previous parliamentary experience. As usual all the government's clients got in, but as in 1658 all their enemies were also eligible to sit and the Upper House had drained off most of the Protectorate's best speakers. As before the regime's representatives did their best to guide debate, both by eloquence and by tactical tricks, but they were hampered by the determination of their republican opponents and by a disinclination upon the part of most MPs to be led. Nonetheless, Richard and most of his councillors were determined to stick the business out as the need for money was so urgent. They allowed the presentation to the Commons of the Commonwealthsmen's petition appealing to the army, which had thrown Oliver Cromwell into a panic a year before, and it seemed to create no stir after all. Slowly the constitution began to work. The MPs recognised the Upper House provided that some of the old hereditary peerage were added, and accepted the Scottish and Irish members. They set about obtaining precise information about the shortfall upon the revenue, and they confirmed the Protector's control over the armed forces. A war had broken out between Denmark and Sweden and the Dutch were intervening in the struggle to strengthen their existing commercial supremacy in the Baltic. It had always been Oliver Cromwell's policy to engage in active diplomacy in that region so that English interests could be defended. His son now developed this policy by sending a fleet thither under Montagu to watch the situation.

Thus the second Lord Protector appeared by early April to be solving the worst of the problems left by the first. Three things were, within weeks, to halt this progress and to destroy the Protectorate: the anxieties of the army, the irresponsibility of the Parliament, and the rashness of Richard Cromwell. During the course of the session the latter's republican enemies bombarded the soldiers with tracts accusing the Protectorate of tending towards revived monarchy, religious intolerance and the destruction of the army itself. Richard decided to convene a Council of Officers to defuse discontent. This seemed to succeed, for the anger and violent language of some of the junior members was opposed by Fleetwood and most of their superiors, and on the 6th the Council of Officers petitioned Parliament only to secure the nation against royalists and to attend to the soldiers' pay. The next day the Commons received the long-awaited report on the revenue. It was now falling short by nearly £330,000 per annum, there were £2½ million worth of debts and the army was owed nearly £890,000 in arrears. An enormous increase in the assessment was obviously needed, but instead the MPs questioned the figures, called Boteler to account for his actions as Major-General and showed favour to royalists. Richard, sensing the anger in the army, decided to destroy its power in politics by a pre-emptive coup. His charm and eloquence had been noted by all civilian observers, but when dealing with military men he had come to rely increasingly upon anger and indignation. This belief in the effectiveness of browbeating the soldiers reached its climax in the events of 18–22 April. First Richard's clients in the Commons got the house to vote that the Council of Officers could sit only with the permission of Parliament and that every officer had to subscribe a declaration against the coercion of Parliaments. Then Richard told the Council that it was dissolved and that its members had to leave London. On the 21st the Commons began debating the settlement of a militia, perhaps to be controlled by themselves. Fleetwood and Disbrowe now demanded the dissolution of Parliament and called the soldiers around London to a rendezvous, whereupon Richard struck back at once by summoning them to him. He then learned, with horror, that the regiments led by colonels loyal to him were marching off to join the mutiny: with the ignorance of an outsider he had assumed that the attitudes of the colonels necessarily determined those of their men. Instead, inadequate pay, the propaganda of the Commonwealthsmen, and perhaps a visceral distrust of Richard Cromwell himself made the common soldiers vote with their boots to end the Parliament and to put the leadership of the nation firmly back with the Council of Officers. The now impotent Protector gave the order for dissolution as the officers demanded, and then the Council set about recasting the government of England.

As in April 1653, so in April 1659, the army had dissolved a Parliament without having an alternative regime to hand, and once again its leaders argued furiously over the form that would be chosen. Even after Richard's principal supporters had been expelled and those officers cashiered by Oliver Cromwell restored, the Council still contained many people, including Fleetwood, who wanted to retain a Protectorate. What prevented this more than anything else, was the opposition to it of the junior officers in town and many of the common soldiers. They clamoured for the restoration of the Purged Parliament, swayed by tracts by Commonwealthsmen promising pay, arrears, religious liberty and swift elections of sympathetic MPs. On 5 May the Council of Officers resolved, in traditional fashion, upon a compromise. It recalled the surviving members of the Purged Parliament on the conditions that they agreed to replace the Protectorate's Council and Upper House with a senate which would include soldiers, to reform the law and the Church, to guarantee the freedom of the independent congregations, to give Richard Cromwell a palace and a pension and then to dissolve themselves having provided for new elections. Richard himself had remained at Whitehall, secretly calling the Scottish and Irish armies to his aid. Monck, however, found that his own junior officers enthusiastically supported the work of their colleagues, and he wrote a fulsome letter of congratulation to the restored MPs. Henry was utterly unprepared to serve the new regime, but he could not persuade an army which now had pay fifteen months in arrear, which depended upon England for some of the money which it did get, and which was outnumbered by the soldiers in the other two countries, to fight for him. So in June he resigned his post and left Ireland. In August Montagu brought back the fleet and retired into private life. Richard had returned, fuming, to the routine of a country squire some three months before. Had he been more of either a soldier or a milksop he would probably not have lost power.

The total number of members left available to serve in the Purged Parliament was seventy-eight, and only sixty-five of these appeared, so that it was in practice even smaller than the Little Parliament of 1653. This all made for the possibility of swifter work, and a series of initiatives were commenced at once. It was soon obvious that the attitudes of the men concerned had altered hardly at all since their expulsion. That event had made them determined not to placate the army but to bring it to heel. At the same time, no more than in the first period of their rule were they willing to enact radical reforms of the sort that many of the soldiers wanted. They began by appointing a Council of State dominated by their own members but including several leaders of the army. They went on, in June, to make the Speaker, not Fleetwood, responsible for commissioning all officers, and used this power to purge the last of Richard Cromwell's supporters and to restore some Commonwealthsmen and Fifth Monarchists. They also replaced the Protectorate's officers of state with commissions of MPs, and ignored the army's request to provide for Richard Cromwell. During the same period they approached the question of reform exactly as they had done before, by debating proposals extensively and doing virtually nothing. They confirmed, stage by stage, exactly the same religious settlement as had been made by the early Protectorate. They favoured the same sort of ministers as those who had influenced that regime most strongly, the independent pastors who believed in a national Church. Their committee on liberty of conscience released a few Quakers from prison and rebuked clergymen who had raised mobs against them, but the House as a whole ordered that tithes be properly paid and tightened the laws against disturbing official church services. Nothing was done to alter the legal system and although it was voted to sit no longer than twelve months, the MPs could not decide upon the form of their successor. Some, like the army, wanted a second House, either appointed or elected, while others were utterly opposed to restrictions upon the authority of the Commons. In one important respect, the restored House was even more dilatory than before, for while in 1649 and 1651 it had raised the assessment to record levels, it now seemed as reluctant to raise taxation as Richard Cromwell's Parliament had been. Thus nothing was done to tackle the gigantic problem of the public finances.

Nonetheless, it is clear that the country in general viewed the restored Commonwealth as a much more radical regime than the Protectorate had been. The accession of Richard Cromwell had been hailed by scores of congratulatory addresses from the rulers of towns and counties and from religious groups. The Purged Parliament upon its return received instead some thirty addresses from sections of communities who wanted reforms of the sort associated with the sects, Fifth Monarchists and Quakers. At the same time the London presses began to pour forth blueprints for such changes in a way not known for ten years. Petitions for the abolition of tithes, promoted by Quakers and containing thousands of signatures, were presented to the MPs. The Parliament remodelled the country's militia commissions to place local defence in its supporters' hands, and in doing so increased fears of radical change. In some counties like Sussex, the return of prominent Commonwealthsmen to power actually increased the domination of affairs by gentry from traditional ruling families. In Buckinghamshire, Devon and Cornwall the presbyterian gentry who had served the Protectorate were not dislodged simply because the Purged Parliament added a few soldiers and sectaries. But in other English counties such as Somerset, and all over Wales, the militia was put in the hands of the most extreme reformers ever to hold power, including Fifth Monarchists and (at Bristol) Quakers. The JPs effectively purged themselves, because so many of the more conservative individuals in commission failed to attend the midsummer sessions in disgust at the alteration in national affairs. The Quakers drew up lists of potential replacements for these men. In Scotland the army was purged by order of Parliament and several of the new officers named were zealous members of religious sects. In Ireland Henry Cromwell was replaced by a team of five noted radicals. These did appoint many Quaker and baptist JPs, and the baptists were soon recovering the dominance which they had once enjoyed in the land under Fleetwood. Yet again, events in the western island were taken by some as presaging the future of England and Wales.

The effect of all this was to raise fear of religious radicals in the English provinces to fever pitch. Rumours of armed takeovers by

Fifth Monarchists or Quakers, mob attacks upon Quaker evangelists and the size and activity of dissident religious groups all increased rapidly. Baptists withdrew from co-operation with presbyterians and independents in some areas in expectation of the approaching destruction of the national Church. Such a situation, in turn, propelled some Civil War parliamentarians who had supported the Protectorate to ally with royalists for a pre-emptive armed rebellion. It was timed for 1 August, and was intended to consist of a multiplicity of local risings which would divide the republic's army and defeat it in detail. The number of people involved made this the most ambitious royalist conspiracy of the decade, but the vigilance of the government in posting soldiers and arresting suspects meant that almost all the projected rebels either failed to stir on the day, or were immediately overpowered, just as in 1655. But this time there was an exception, in Cheshire, where Sir George Booth, a former parliamentarian and presbyterian and a very respected local leader, gained control of that county and the adjacent parts of Lancashire and North Wales. This provided what Charles II had been hoping for since his alliance with Spain, a bridgehead through which a Spanish army might enter and restore him to the throne. But there were no Spanish regiments available, as the government in Madrid was now only interested in making peace with France and rebuilding its finances. So Booth could only remain in Cheshire until a task force of the Commonwealth's army arrived there and destroyed his band on 19 August at Winnington Bridge. A week later all his fortresses had surrendered and the rebellion was over.

It seemed to many, now, that the second English Revolution, the abolition of the state Church and of lawyers and the codification of the law, was about to begin. The royalists and presbyterians were utterly crushed, their presses silent, while radical writers demanded reforms with a new confidence and urgency. Charles II had given up all hope of activity on his behalf in England and Wales in the near future. The way in which the gathered churches and some Quakers had rallied to the Commonwealth's defence during the rebellion made it seem more likely that the Purged Parliament would accede to their wishes. The MPs did exonerate the dead John Lilburne and release the Quaker James Naylor, who had given such offence to the Second Protectorate Parliament. On 16 September the task force of soldiers which had broken Booth sent a petition to Westminster accusing the restored members of dilatoriness and ingratitude and demanding 'godly reform'. The proponents of such reform wrote and campaigned with as much vigour as those who had been active ten years before, but they now had a larger and more widely distributed basis of popular support in the greater number of gathered churches and in the Quaker movement. The British Republic had always been a centrifuge, the forces of further reform pulling against those of reaction, but during 1659 the tug had become more frenzied than ever before and it seemed that the radicals were winning.

What prevented the swift implementation of a victory was the perennial inability of the radicals themselves to agree upon a common blueprint for a government. Both inside the Purged Parliament and the army officer corps, some wanted a select assembly of 'saints' and others were just as determined to secure representative bodies elected by the public, though with safe-guards to ensure that the right people got elected. A range of hybrid forms was debated, during September and October, without any sign of prospective agreement. What aborted all projects, and ultimately destroyed the Commonwealth was, however, a different sort of division among the radical leaders, the struggle for supremacy between Parliament and army. Both were determined to control the other and during the summer the MPs had tended to get the better of the contest. They were only permitted to do so because the soldiers were conscious of the fact that they might soon have to face a rebellion. Within a couple of weeks of the surrender of Booth's last stronghold, the army had set about trying to reassert its wishes. The strongest personality within it was now John Lambert, who had been restored to his command by the Council of Officers a week before they called back the Purged Parliament. It was an ominous association of actions, for the handsome and flamboyant Lambert, a soldier, aesthete and statesman, was the very individual who had created the Protectorate and consistently represented the controlling interest of the military in public affairs. He was welcomed back to service by the ordinary soldiers with wild delight, and commanded the force which won the action at Winnington Bridge. It was this same force which rounded on Parliament in September, by sending up a petition demanding reform. But the other clauses of the petition created a greater stir at Westminster, for they included demands for a 'senate' to limit the powers of the Commons, for the bestowal of the rank of general upon all its leaders, and for the promise which Oliver Cromwell had refused to give in 1658, that no officer be dismissed except by a court martial.

Lambert was not present when this document was drafted, and the stridency of its tone makes it sound very much like a genuine compilation by the junior officers. Nevertheless, many MPs suspected the work of the army leaders and there followed an angry debate, not about whether to accept the petition but about whether to punish the initiators. In the end they were rebuked, whereupon the army's Council of Officers reconvened and responded with a protest at this treatment and a request for the concession concerning court martials. Lambert, Disbrowe, Berry and six other senior commanders then sent out a letter requesting units in the provinces to subscribe this new petition. There was nothing illegal about this, but when the MPs heard of it on 12 October they misunderstood it as an intention to employ force against themselves, and their nerve, patience and common sense all shattered. They voted the nine signatories out of their commissions and summoned supposedly loyal regiments to assist them. What followed was a repetition of Richard Cromwell's attempted coup. Almost all the common soldiers answered Lambert's commands, and on the next day the army's leaders closed up the House of Commons once again and left the Commonwealth without a government.

Once again, the army had acted precipitately, without any notion of a replacement for the regime which it had expelled. But this time the difficulties which it faced were far more serious. It had acted not to secure reform or even nominally to defend the public interest, but purely to save the careers of some of its leaders. The stark selfishness of the move dismayed and divided the civilian radicals who had traditionally been the soldiers' main allies. The junior officers now clamoured for the immediate abolition of tithes and of Chancery, but the Council of Officers were as reluctant as ever to impose such sweeping reforms without the authority of a Parliament or at least of a body of civilians. As a result, some of the sects and Quakers turned to the Council and lobbied it for radical changes, while many of their colleagues, and the independent congregations who approved of the national Church, remained idle. The officers appointed a Committee of Safety to run the country, consisting of their own leaders plus a greater number of civilian collaborators who turned out mostly to be time-servers instead of reformers. These people were no more likely to succeed in agreeing swiftly upon a new constitution than the expelled MPs had been. At the time of the expulsion the Purged Parliament had only just been commencing the work of raising the assessment, so that the arrears of the armies in all three kingdoms had continued to mount through the summer. Unless the Committee of Safety produced writs for a Parliament very soon, which was unlikely, there was no prospect of anything except a further deterioration in the situation. The renewed activity of Spanish privateers and war in the Baltic were causing a serious fall in the customs receipts and increasing economic recession and unemployment. But all these problems were peripheral to the greatest one faced by Lambert and his colleagues, that for the first time the army itself had divided and seemed about to fight itself.

The division was along the Scottish border for, upon hearing news of the expulsion of the Parliament, George Monck had declared resolutely against the action and purged his officer corps of all who disagreed with him. The fact that he had been left in control of Scotland was an anomaly, for he was the only one of the Cromwellians who had supported a more conservative turn to the Protectorate to survive the fall of that regime. The Purged Parliament had found his fulsome letters to it sufficiently convincing, and his rule of the northern realm sufficiently impressive, to leave him in office at a time when rebellion was brewing and they needed his abilities. It was his relative conservatism which seems to have precipitated his action, for during the summer he had apparently become convinced that radical reform, especially the destruction of the Church of England, was likely. When the Purged Parliament was expelled in October, he believed that the last barrier to such changes, the prospect of which appalled him, had gone and he acted precipitately to halt the process. His task was an extremely difficult one. The whole of the army in England had rallied to its leaders except the garrison of Hull, which remained neutral. The troops in Ireland declared their solidarity with them. Monck only secured the co-operation of his own men by touring their quarters with a task force of loyal soldiers and arresting opponents. In the end he had to cashier or face the desertion of over a hundred officers, and his efforts to replace them were hampered by his stubborn refusal to employ any of the Scots. Lambert collected a marching army and brought it up to Newcastle to face him in mid-November. But time was on Monck's side. It was winter, and a campaign into Scotland would be difficult to mount. The Committee of Safety at London was only too happy to hold back Lambert for weeks while they talked to Monck's representatives, sincerely believing that agreement could be reached without bloodshed. The soldiers at Newcastle were reluctant to attack their comrades. Monck's men were relatively well-paid because Scotland was still overtaxed in comparison with England and because he had been sent a large subvention from London in the summer when rebellion was feared. Lambert's soldiers, by contrast, were soon receiving virtually no pay at all and some had worn out their shoes.

But George Monck's greatest advantage was that his example was inspiring the army's enemies in England, while he had drawn off its most dynamic leader and its finest men to the Border. In early December serious rioting broke out among the London apprentices, young men who had grown up under the republic and viewed it not as a delivery from oppression but the embodiment of that quality. The removal of most soldiers from the city to face Monck, and the deepening economic depression, caused them to voice their resentment in a demand for a 'free' Parliament, the membership of which would be controlled neither by soldiers nor by Commonwealthsmen. The Portsmouth garrison mutinied for lack of pay and declared for the Purged Parliament, whereupon the navy did the same and blockaded the Thames. More units followed their example, and on 23 December the Council of Officers dissolved to try to arrest the process, having failed to agree upon the form of an alternative government. There never would be another such Council. The following day the soldiers left around London ignored their commanders and invited the Purged Parliament to resume its seats, as the only body likely to deliver firm government and pay the army. Lambert tried to march south to reverse this development, but his now almost starving soldiers deserted in droves as he moved. By the last day of December the Commonwealthsmen appeared to have achieved what had been a dream to them for twelve years, the securing of real control over the army in England.

Their victory meant the absolute end to any chance that further radical reform would occur, because the people who had supported the army leadership during the previous few months had tended to be those who had wanted such reform. They were purged from Parliament, turning it into an even more 'moderate' or 'conservative' body in comparison with the Quakers and sects. They were also removed from the militia, while three-eighths of the entire army officer corps was replaced, including half the field officers and two-thirds of the captains. Fleetwood, Disbrowe and Lambert went, but also most of the soldiers who had clamoured for reform in the previous year. They were replaced by newcomers, men who had supported Richard Cromwell in his attempted coup, and men who had been dismissed in 1647–8 for wishing to come to terms with Charles I. To provide security while this process went on, the MPs invited their greatest champion, George Monck, to accept the post of Commander-in-Chief and to march his army south to London. He had followed Lambert down to York and then, having supervised the dispersal of his enemy's regiments, halted to await further orders. Now he and his men were summoned to the centre of national affairs. Behind him he left a Scotland which was still patrolled by English soldiers but where, before his march, he had entrusted local civilian government to county committees composed of Scots. As a result, the latter now had more control of their own affairs than at any previous time since the English conquest. In Ireland the clock had been turned back also, but towards 1658 not 1650. As the English army divided and disowned its leaders in December, that in Ireland grew still more demoralised, and more badly paid as the subventions from England ceased. As a result it made little resistance when a group of 'Old Protestants' (pre-civil war English settlers) arrested the government put in by the Purged Parliament. The leaders of the coup were people such as Broghil, who had faithfully served Henry Cromwell and supported his more conservative religious and political policies. Now they followed up their victory by ejecting the baptists and Quakers from office.

Thus, in all three realms, the Commonwealth was now based upon groups of people whose attitudes were more, instead of less, conservative or reactionary than those of the central government. By purging the army in England, the now twice-restored Parliament had removed most of the soldiers who had a personal commitment to the beliefs which had brought about the English Revolution in the first place. This fact was not lost upon a large number, perhaps the majority, of the English public, who took up the London apprentices' cry for a 'free' Parliament with tremendous gusto. Between the return of the Purged House and the end of January, the apprentices of Exeter demonstrated for this cause, and gentry in ten counties produced declarations or petitions either for a 'free' Parliament or for the readmission of the members removed at Pride's Purge. The Purged Parliament now became known by its enduring nickname of 'The Rump'. The majority of the Parliament, however, showed no sign of concern at this state of affairs. It appointed a new Council of State dominated by hard-line republicans such as Hesilrige. It declared that the national Church (supported by tithes) and the freedom of gathered congregations to worship were both sacrosanct in law. It began to dispose of the financial problem by raising the assessment upon all three realms together to £100,000 per month. It voted to fill itself up with new members very swiftly. And it placed its faith in Monck's approaching army to secure it against all disturbances.

Significantly, it was to that same general that most of those agitating for an alteration in the nature of the regime directed their appeals. For George Monck was a complex figure. He was a renegade royalist who had stuck loyally to the Cromwells as long as they could be powerful patrons to him, and then deftly jettisoned their cause in order to save his career. In this sense he was an opportunist. Yet he had also risked everything to save the national Church, and each time that he had expressed personal opinions or instincts, they had been in favour of a more conservative settlement than that embodied in the Commonwealth. Contemporaries who met Monck after crediting him with tremendous intelligence and power of vision were always surprised by the coarse, jovial, hard-drinking, swarthy-jowled character whom they encountered. His strength was that he was patient, thorough, cunning and (save for his single swift reaction in October 1659) tended to adapt carefully to events. Upon his march south in January he behaved like an exemplary servant of the Purged Parliament. But when he arrived in London on 2 February he found almost the entire city in turmoil, from the Common Council downwards, disowning the authority of that Parliament. Apprentice riots broke out at Bristol and Gloucester, and five more counties and two cities produced petitions for a 'free' Parliament or the reversal of Pride's Purge. The reply of the MPs was to order Monck to repress the agitation among Londoners. The command went against the advice of his wife, his chaplain, his entire officer corps and some members of the Purged House itself, and doubtless against his own instincts as well. It is not surprising that, having initially obeyed the command, on the 11th he criticised the behaviour of the House and ten days later he reversed Pride's Purge, by readmitting the survivors of those members who had been removed in December 1648. For the first time, soldiers enforced the entry of people to a Parliament instead of their exit from one. But they still guarded the locked door of the House of Lords.

During his rule over Scotland, Monck's policy had been to stabilise the country by gaining the middle ground of political opinion while maintaining order with his army. This was, in effect, what he was doing in England now. The readmitted MPs, who now formed a majority of the House, were allowed back only on condition that they established a presbyterian national Church with toleration of separatist groups, made Monck Commander-in-Chief of the armed forces, and proceeded to a speedy dissolution. To soothe republican opinion among the army units scattered through the provinces, and among civilians, he warned the enlarged House publicly of the destructive effects of a restored monarchy. To cow soldiers who might have protested, he ensured that the various regiments were bombarded with propaganda in favour of his actions, and dismissed two colonels who had been notable Fifth Monarchists. The enlarged Parliament faithfully carried out all of the three tasks which he had set it, although not without much debate and some hesitation, and dissolved itself on 16 March. It also confirmed the heavy new assessment to pay the armies, and passed an act to transfer leadership of the county militia bands to those members of the traditional local elites who had not been royalists. In this manner the minor gentry and commoners who had served the republican regimes were at last swept from power.

The departing MPs had provided for a new Parliament to meet on 25 April. It was likely to settle the fate of all three realms, for Scotland was still completely passive and the 'Old Protestants' of Ireland were waiting upon events at Westminster. They had convened a national assembly, which represented the Protestant settlers of their country, in February. This did act decisively to reintroduce the system of church government devised under Henry Cromwell, as a rough parallel to the tolerant presbyterianism projected for England, but it deferred all political decisions until the direction of events at Westminster had become more clear. What that direction would be was already fairly likely before the end of March. The popular acclamation of Monck's moves in February had been thunderous. Thirty-one bonfires could be seen from a single bridge over the Thames upon the night after he turned upon the Commonwealthsmen. The news was carried across the country to a clamour of bells and a flaring of many more fires. Royalist toasts were drunk by crowds in the capital on the evening upon which the enlarged parliament was dissolved. The writs for the new one did specify that none of the King's old adherents or their sons could seek election, and (apart from the lack of members from Scotland and Ireland) promised to produce a House not very different from the Protectorate's Parliaments. On the other hand, Quakers were now disqualified from voting, and in practice so many royalists ignored the prohibition that they or their sons represented sixty-one of the members eventually returned. The Commonwealthsmen fared atrociously, and most of the former officers of the army of England did not try to stand. The majority of the Convention Parliament, as it became termed, were difficult to categorise in terms of a previous record. But they were substantial gentry who were most unlikely to favour a Commonwealth.

To Charles II and his exiled courtiers, still living in the Spanish Netherlands, these developments appeared virtually incredible. The failure of Booth's Rebellion had appeared to exhaust the present possibilities of royalist activity within Britain, while the run-down of Spain's war with the British Republic had ended hopes of a restoration by Spanish arms. The ejection of the Purged Parliament in October had slightly revived the exiles' hopes, only for its return to blight them once more. Suddenly, from February, events began to run swiftly towards a recall of the King to his throne. It is likely that both General Monck and Charles II realised at the same moment, in early March, that it was wise to start negotiating against such a possibility. Soon after the dissolution of the Parliament, they made a secret exchange, which Monck insisted should be purely verbal. The general asked the terms which his own officers had already decided upon as the basis for any settlement of the country and which were confined to the material needs of their army-indemnity, arrears of pay, confirmation of the new owner-ship of former Church and Crown land, and a measure of toleration of religious dissent. The readmitted MPs had, before their dissolution, reappointed Oliver Cromwell's favourite naval commander, Montagu, to command the fleet. His refusal to serve the Commonwealth and his identification with the reactionary element on the Cromwells' Council both recommended him to the MPs and indicated his possible willingness to accept Charles. This view was correct, for by early April he had been contacted by a royalist agent and offered loyalty to assist a Stuart restoration. In the same weeks secret messages expressing support began to flow into the exiled court from various leading politicians in England and Ireland who perceived the probable trend of events. By the middle of April, when all the returns for the Convention were in, it was very likely that Charles II would be invited back to England by that body, unless either the royalists behaved with wanton stupidity or the republicans intervened with armed force.

The first of these did not occur, but the second did. The exiled court begged its traditional supporters in England to express forgiveness and conciliation to their old enemies. The royalists responded with nine declarations from different counties and from the London area, signed by an impressive number of nobles and gentry and forswearing any revenge upon the people who had fought them in the Civil Wars and persecuted them during the Interregnum. Republicans were also busy publishing, not declarations but tracts aimed at filling the soldiers of the various scattered army units with fear of a royal restoration. The crisis came on 10 April, when Lambert escaped from preventive detention in the Tower of London and called all supporters of a republic to arms. He was ignored by Hesilrige, Fleetwood, Disbrowe and most of the former leaders of army and state, but soldiers from at least six horse regiments rode to join him, two castles declared for him and risings by civilians occurred or were attempted in at least nine counties. This show of support is all the more impressive in view of the measures taken previously by Monck and the caretaker Council of State left by the MPs readmitted to the Purged Parliament. The army had been bombarded with government propaganda to persuade it to submit to the wishes of the Convention and toured by a strike force instructed to root out the disaffected. The City of London supplied loans to keep it properly paid, and more of its senior officers were replaced. The militia was raised under its new gentry officers. Thus the vigour which remained among many republicans was remarkable, but their failure was still virtually inevitable. The nucleus of Lambert's rebel army was attacked at Edgehill on the 22nd by a unit of Monck's, and he himself was recaptured as his splendid Arab horse got stuck in a ploughed field. After that, the other republican bands could be hunted down separately, and within a week all was over.

Even as the mopping-up operation was being carried out, on 25 April, the Convention Parliament met to commence the obsequies of the republic. The House of Lords was reoccupied immediately, first by former parliamentarian peers and then by those who had come of age during the 1650s. The Commons recognised their right to sit, and Monck accepted this judgement. Both Houses then adjourned to await a proposal from Charles II, and on May Day it was delivered in the form of the Declaration of Breda. The joint work of Charles and his three most favoured advisers, it deftly referred to the Parliament itself the settlement of the questions of indemnity, confiscated crown and church lands, the army's arrears and the confirmation of the existing degree of religious liberty. At that, the Houses voted that the government of England was by King, Lords and Commons, and the British Republic formally came to an end. An army had created it, against the corporate will of the nation, and it ended as soon as the army, after a fashion, changed its mind.

CONCLUSION

A superficially good case could be made that the Interregnum was one of the least significant periods of English history. The years between 1640 and 1648 shattered the Tudor and early Stuart State and Church beyond repair, produced what was probably the nation's biggest and bloodiest civil war, and germinated a set of new ideas and speculations. They removed the Crown's traditional prerogative courts, such as Star Chamber, High Commission and the Council of the North, for ever. They replaced the decayed system of Tudor taxation with a more efficient means of valuation, and lent such enhanced importance to Parliaments that they would henceforth play a major part in all political calculations. And they permanently ended the ability of the Church of England to attract the allegiance of virtually all English Protestants, creating dissent upon a large and permanent scale. The years between 1660 and 1662 established a working model of relationships between Crown, Church, Parliament and local elites which was finally to be achieved in 1688–1701 to produce the relative stability of the eighteenth-century English polity. In this perspective the Interregnum appears as a limbo or a blind alley, rather a waste of time, from which only the possession of Jamaica emerges as a solid gain. The readmission of the Jews and the passage of the first Navigation Act, it might be argued, would have occurred sooner or later under any regime.

There is one simple answer to this viewpoint: that had the

army not intervened to wrench Parliament from its preferred course in 1648, a very different settlement would have been achieved from that which was enacted in the early 1660s. There would have been a much weaker Crown, making the actual course of late-seventeenth-century English history impossible. There would have been a presbyterian Church, and dissent in 1648 was still limited enough to have been crushed out of existence altogether. The ruling elite would have been divided more bitterly and perhaps more lengthily than the Whigs and Tories were to be under the early Hanoverians. The Interregnum had the historical equivalent to the effect which is observed in medicine, of holding open the edges of a wound long enough to leave a permanent scar. It ensured that the congregational independents and the baptists and other sects could multiply sufficiently to ensure their survival when an intolerant national Church was restored. It enabled the Quakers, Diggers, Fifth Monarchists and yet more radical thinkers to emerge, all making important contributions to the history of ideas, and the first establishing a permanent presence. It ensured that the social elite would become sufficiently convinced of the importance of pomp, hierarchy and ceremony to ensure that the Church would be ruled by bishops and filled with rituals thereafter. The sporadic but significant interest of many gentry and parish elites in improving the manners and morals of commoners died away with the Interregnum, as reform had acquired unpleasantly radical connotations and religious dissent became a greater problem. Above all, the execution of the King, at the insistence of an army which spanned the social spectrum, administered an infinitely greater shock to the English (and to the social elite in particular) than the Civil Wars had done. It made the landowning class determined as never before to control its world, putting the Crown, the Church, the dissenters and the urban corporations as far as possible in its power so that stability could thus be guaranteed. This was what the Restoration Settlements of 1660–2 were intended to achieve, and what was indeed to be secured after 1688. The enduring impact of the Revolution and its aftermath upon the English imagination can be seen in the drama of the 1660s and 1670s. The playwrights of those decades turned again and again to the questions of usurpation, collaboration, loyalty and deceit. In politics as in love, they felt themselves to be living in a world where familiar boundaries had all been broken and nothing could be trusted any more.

Nonetheless, it is in a British, not an English, context that the true importance of the Interregnum should be appreciated. It is not too much of an exaggeration to suggest that during the years 1649–53 the modern political relationships of the three British realms were formed. In 1660 they divided once more into three kingdoms, theoretically linked only by a crown, but there is little doubt that the balance between them had been determined by the events of the previous decade in a way that had not been done before. It was Cromwell's army which ensured that henceforth England would be clearly dominant over the other two realms. In the period 1640–6 the Scottish government had intervened successfully to impose its wishes upon English affairs, and in 1648–51 it attempted to repeat this intervention with great determination. After 1651 the administrations based in Edinburgh never aspired to such an ambition, being content at most to try to manipulate the divisions at Westminster. The test of the new relationship came in 1689, when the Scots on the whole tended to take their measures from English developments. In this sense the permanent Union of 1707 had been presaged from the moment that the battle of Worcester was won. In Ireland the Catholic uprising of 1641 had destroyed the possibility that the land might be owned and governed by a mixture of Catholics and Protestants, undergoing a slow process of political assimilation. It was the war of 1649–53 which ensured that instead it would be dominated for nearly three centuries by Protestants of English extraction ruling with the assistance of English arms. It also ensured that Irish Catholic commoners would be turned into a helot class instead of cultural, religious and social replicas of the English. In one sense the British Republic was a brief and unsuccessful experiment. In another, the entire archipelago has never recovered from its remoulding by the people who executed Charles I.

Notes

1. A feature of this book which may strike some readers as eccentric is my desire to avoid reproducing traditional names for institutions which are not themselves contemporary and are partisan, abusive or inappropriate. Thus, I shall consistently refer to the Parliament created by Pride's Purge as the Purged Parliament, and not as the Rump or Rump Parliament. The latter terms were not employed for it until 1659, and were, of course, coined by its enemies. Similarly, Barebone's or the Barebones Parliament will in due course be called the Little Parliament in these pages.
2. This information is taken from a paper read by Ian Gentles at Cambridge in 1983. When Professor Gentles publishes his book upon the army then a lot of our ignorance about it will be dispelled.
3. See *A Modest Narrative* (21–28 April 1649), p. 31, and (5–11 May 1649), p. 44; *Mercurius Pragmaticus* (23–30 April 1649), p. A3; *The Moderate* (1–8 May 1649), p. W2; *The Unanimous Declaration of Colonel Scroope's and Commissary General Ireton's Regiments* (11 May 1649).
4. He walked off with it and it was never seen again.
5. Churchwardens' papers for this period are not, as has sometimes been suggested, an indication of the kind of service provided. A Prayer Book listed in an inventory may not have been opened: conversely, one in use may not have been listed. A Directory purchased and employed by a minister would not feature in the accounts.
6. Based on the records in Public Record Office, S.P.22.
7. *Kingdom's Weekly Intelligencer* (19 April 1649), p. 1334.
8. This is not true of Warwickshire, but inspection of the manuscript

sources for Wiltshire and those published for other counties suggests that Warwickshire was the exception, possessing an unusually popular and determined set of new rulers.

9. The sources are listed quite accurately in Samuel Rawson Gardiner, *History of the Commonwealth and Protectorate* (1903), i.112–24, 127–33.

10. Further evidence upon this issue is contained in two remarkable unpublished theses: Henry Reece, 'The Military Presence in England, 1649–1660' (Oxford D.Phil., 1981), and Richard Williams, 'County and Municipal Government in Cornwall, Devon, Dorset and Somerset 1649–1660' (Bristol Ph.D., 1982). The former is justly celebrated among historians but the latter deserves more attention.

11. This is how I make sense of the problem and of the sources dealt with slightly differently in J.F. MaGregor's essay, 'Ranterism and the Development of English Quakerism', *Journal of Religious History*, 9 (1976–7), 349–63, and my own question as to how in 1659 so many outsiders could describe as Quakers people whose activities do not feature at all in the Swarthmore Papers and First Publishers of Truth.

12. These were printed accurately but with a misleading gloss by C. H. Firth (who attributes them to Montagu) in *The Clarke Papers*, vol. iii (Camden Society, 1899), pp. 203–8. I have used the originals, preserved among the Sandwich Papers at Mapperton House, Dorset. I am extremely grateful to Victor Montagu, Esq., for his kindness and hospitality upon that occasion, and also to the Hon. John Montagu for arranging my visit and to Felix Pryor, Esq., for effecting the initial introduction.

13. These are proposed in five policy documents which were removed to Ugbrooke Park, Devon, by the 1st Baron Clifford in 1673. I read them there, but in 1987 they were sold to a private buyer. At the time of writing the British Library may be negotiating for their acquisition. I am profoundly grateful to the present Baron and Baroness for their friendship upon that and many another occasion.

BIBLIOGRAPHY

All titles named are published in London unless otherwise stated.

The only detailed overall survey of part of the period to be published in recent years is Ronald Hutton, *The Restoration* (Oxford, 1985), which covers the years 1658 to 1660 in its first section. For the earlier part of the Interregnum, we still have to use Samuel R. Gardiner, *History of the Commonwealth and Protectorate* (1897), 4 vols, and Sir Charles H. Firth, *The Last Years of the Protectorate* (1909), 2 vols. Together they remain our basic narratives for the years 1649 to 1658 because of their wealth of factual detail. Also (unlike *The Restoration*) they do cover the entire British Isles.

It is clear enough that the motor force of central politics in the period was the army, but no proper study of this organisation during the Interregnum has been published since Sir Charles H. Firth, *Cromwell's Army* (1902, reprinted as a University paperback 1967). Important new evidence has been presented in theses by Henry Reece and Derek Massarella, but neither of these is likely to be published. Ian Gentles is preparing an important book upon the army up to 1653 (see note 2), but until it appears all that we have are passages in the works by Gardiner, Firth and Hutton, above, and by Worden and Woolrych, below, and a clutch of articles: C. Polizzotto, 'Liberty of Conscience and the Whitehall Debates', *Journal of Ecclesiastical History* (1975); and B. Taft, 'The Humble Petition of Several Colonels of the Army', *Huntingdon Library Quarterly* (1978–9), 'Voting Lists of the Council of Officers, December 1648', *Bulletin of the Institute of Historical Research* (1979), and 'The Council of Officers' Agreement of the People', *Historical Journal* (1985).

The Parliaments of the period have been much better served, so that we have at present A. B. Worden, *The Rump Parliament* (Cambridge,

138

1974); Austin Woolrych, *Commonwealth to Protectorate* (Oxford, 1982), which is mostly concerned with the Little Parliament; P. Gaunt, 'Law-Making in the First Protectorate Parliament', in *Politics and People in Revolutionary England*, edited by Colin Jones, Malyn Newitt and Stephen Roberts (Oxford, 1986); and D. Hirst, 'Concord and Discord in Richard Cromwell's House of Commons', *English Historical Review* (1988). There are also many insights into central politics in general in the books by Worden and Woolrych, and in those by Gardiner, Firth and Hutton named above. Peter Gaunt has written an important thesis upon the Councils of the Protectorate which badly needs publication. Nonetheless, there is no modern account of the central politics of the period 1654–8, and a fresh look at the Second Protectorate Parliament and the kingship crisis is definitely needed.

None of the really important figures of the period is represented by a first-class biography, not even Cromwell himself. The essays edited by Ivan Roots as *Cromwell: A Profile* (1973) are the most useful modern work on the Protector and his government, though John Morrill has just edited and sent to press what will probably be an even finer collection by different contributors. Charles P. Korr, *Cromwell and the New Model Foreign Policy* (1975) makes a study of an aspect of Oliver's 'reign'. We need new studies of Lambert, Monck, Thurloe, Hesilrige and Ireton. The well-researched recent biographies tend to be of people who were slightly less influential, such as Violet A. Rowe, *Sir Henry Vane the Younger* (1970), and Ruth Spalding, *The Improbable Puritan* (1975), which is a life of Whitelocke.

The national Church of the Interregnum is also rather badly served, the main authorities still being W. A. Shaw, *A History of the English Church during the Civil Wars and the Commonwealth* (1900), vol. ii, and Thomas Richards, *Religious Developments in Wales 1654–1662* (1923). Useful modern additions to the framework laid down in these are Claire Cross, 'The Church in England 1646–60', in G. E. Aylmer (ed.), *The Interregnum* (1972); R. O'Day and A. Hughes, 'Augmentation and Amalgamation' in *Princes and Paupers in the English Church 1500–1800* (ed. by Rosemary O'Day and Felicity Heal, Leicester, 1981); and R. Clark, 'A Good and Sufficient Maintenance', *Derbyshire Archaeological Journal* (1980).

By contrast, the various dissenting groups have received a huge amount of attention in recent decades. Upon the Catholics there have been J. C. H. Aveling, *The Handle and the Axe* (1976), and T. S. Smith, 'The Persecution of Staffordshire Roman Catholic Recusants 1625–1660', *Journal of Ecclesiastical History* (1979). On the intransigent episcopalians, Robert S. Bosher, *The Making of the Restoration Settlement* (1951); John W. Packer, *The Transformation of Anglicanism*

1643–1660 (Manchester, 1969); and Victor D. Sutch, *Gilbert Sheldon* (The Hague, 1973). On the 'congregational independents', Geoffrey F. Nuttall, *Visible Saints* (1957); Peter Toon, *God's Statesman* (1971); and S. Cook, 'The Congregational Independents and the Cromwellian Constitutions', *Church History* (1977). On the sects, B. S. Capp, *The Fifth Monarchy Men* (1972) and Murray Tolmie, *The Triumph of the Saints* (Cambridge, 1977). On the Quakers, Barry Reay, *The Quakers and the English Revolution* (1985) replaces and takes account of a large amount of earlier work, though William C. Braithwaite, *The Beginnings of Quakerism* (2nd edition, Cambridge, 1961) still provides the basic factual narrative. Christopher Hill, *The World Turned Upside Down* (1972) remains an exciting and provocative survey of radical thinkers, even if its assertions are coming to seem increasingly dubious. *Radical Religion in the English Revolution* (ed. by Barry Reay and J. F. MaGregor, 1984) is a much better and updated overall view. *The World of the Muggletonians* (ed. by Christopher Hill, Barry Reay and William Lamont, 1983) provides a concise guide to recent work upon one sect which has left a marvellous archive.

In the history of ideas and of political pressure groups in the period, also, there is a pronounced emphasis upon radicals. A balanced overview is provided by G. E. Aylmer in his three lectures 'Collective Mentalities in Mid Seventeenth-Century England', in the *Transactions of the Royal Historical Society* (1986–8). Blair Worden has made some notable contributions to the history of political debate with his essays 'Classical Republicanism and the Puritan Revolution' in *History and Imagination* (ed. by Worden, Hugh Lloyd-Jones and Valerie Pearl, 1981); 'The Politics of Marvell's *Horatian Ode*', *Historical Journal* (1984); 'Toleration and the Cromwellian Protectorate', in *Studies in Church History* (1984); 'Providence and Politics in Cromwellian England', *Past and Present* (1985); and 'Literature and Political Censorship in Early Modern England', in *Too Mighty To Be Free* (ed. by Alastair Duke and C. Tamse, 1988). Also important is G. Burgess, 'Usurpation, Obligation and Obedience in the Thought of the Engagement Controversy', *Historical Journal* (1986).

The best recent guide to radical ideologies is F. D. Dow, *Radicalism in the English Revolution* (1986). For more detailed reading there exists a large quantity of good work upon most of the groups. For the Levellers, M. A. Gibb, *John Lilburne* (1947), and Joseph Frank, *The Levellers* (1955) are still useful detailed texts, while G. E. Aylmer, *The Levellers in the English Revolution* (1975) provides an excellent short introduction to a collection of Leveller writings. There are also a trio of essays in the periodical *Past and Present*: J. Davis, 'The Levellers and Democracy' (1968); R. Howell and D. Brewster, 'Reconsidering the

Levellers' (1970); and G. Aylmer, 'Gentlemen Levellers?' (1970). To these should be added I. Gentles, 'London Levellers in the English Revolution', *Journal of Ecclesiastical History* (1978); and N. Carlin, 'Leveller Organisation in London', *Historical Journal* (1984). The Diggers are served by George H. Sabine, *The Works of Gerrard Winstanley* (1965); Christopher Hill's introduction to Gerrard Winstanley, *The Law of Freedom* (1973); J. Alsop, 'Gerrard Winstanley; Religion and Respectability', *Historical Journal* (1985); and the inevitable clutch of essays in *Past and Present*, G. Aylmer, *Englands Spirit Unfoulded* (1968); K. Thomas, 'Another Digger Broadside' and 'The Date of Gerrard Winstanley's *Fire in the Bush*' (1969); J. Davis, 'Gerrard Winstanley and the Restoration of True Magistracy (1976); C. Hill, 'The Religion of Gerrard Winstanley' (Supplement, 1976); J. Alsop, 'Gerrard Winstanley's Later Life' (1979); and the debate upon 'The Religion of Gerrard Winstanley' (1980). All earlier work upon the Ranters must now be reconsidered following the challenge thrown down by J. C. Davis, *Fear, Myth and History* (1986). The first reply to it to have been published is G. Aylmer, 'Did the Ranters exist?' *Past and Present* (1987).

The royalists are considered in Aylmer's second essay in the *Transactions of the Royal Historical Society*, cited above. Paul Hardacre, *The Royalists during the Puritan Revolution* (The Hague, 1956) is patchy but not yet improved upon. David Underdown, *Royalist Conspiracy in England 1649–1660* (1960) will probably never need replacement. A new study of the Stuart court in exile is made in Ronald Hutton's biography of Charles II, due to be published in October 1989.

Ironically, the field of local history, which was comparatively neglected by professional historians until recently, is now better served by them for this period than central politics. At present three studies tower over the rest: Stephen Roberts, *Recovery and Restoration in an English County: Devon Local Administration 1646–70* (1985); Andrew Coleby, *Central Government and the Localities: Hampshire 1649–1689* (Cambridge, 1987); and Ann Hughes, *Politics, Society and Civil War in Warwickshire, 1620–1660* (Cambridge, 1987). But these build upon the following, each one of which set a new standard in its time: J. Round, 'Colchester and the Commonwealth', *English Historical Review* (1900); B. Henderson. 'The Commonwealth Charters', *Transactions of the Royal Historical Society* (1912); C. Parsloe, 'The Corporation of Bedford 1647–1664', in ibid (1947); Mary Coate, *Cornwall in the Great Civil War and Interregnum* (Oxford, 1933); Alan Everitt, *The Community of Kent and the Great Rebellion* (1966); David Underdown, *Somerset in the Civil War and Interregnum* (Newton Abbot, 1973); J. S. Morrill, *Cheshire 1630–1660* (Oxford, 1974); C. Phillips, 'County Committees and Local Government in Cumberland and Westmorland', *Northern*

History (1970), and 'The Royalist North', *Northern History* (1978); A. M. Johnson, 'Wales during the Commonwealth and Protectorate', in *Puritans and Revolutionaries* (ed. by D. H. Pennington and K. V. Thomas, 1978); John T. Evans, *Seventeenth Century Norwich* (Oxford, 1979); Anthony Fletcher, *A County Community in Peace and War: Sussex 1600–1660* (1975); and Clive Holmes, *Seventeenth Century Lincolnshire* (Lincoln, 1980). There are also now three important essays in *Politics and People in Revolutionary England* (ed. by Jones, Newitt and Roberts, cited above): A. Fletcher, 'Oliver Cromwell and the Localities'; P. Pickney, 'The Suffolk Elections to the Protectorate Parliaments'; and S. Roberts, 'Godliness and Government in Glamorgan'.

All these studies to some degree combine considerations of central as well as local government, but there are a few which combine the two with more equal emphasis: David Underdown, *Pride's Purge* (Oxford, 1971) which is a tremendous work on politics in general during 1648–9; S. Roberts, 'Local Government Reform in England and Wales during the Interregnum', in Ivan Roots (ed.) *Into Another Mould* (Exeter, 1981); and C. Polizzotto, 'The Campaign against the Humble Proposals of 1652', *Journal of Ecclesiastical History* (1987). There remain, despite all this mass of work, some notable gaps, and not all of these are due to lack of evidence. Wiltshire has superb records, some of which have been employed for this book, but there is no proper study of it. The Ridings of Yorkshire are also well provided, and C. Foster has employed these archives for 'County Government in Yorkshire during the Interregnum', *Northern History* (1976). But although this is an important essay, much more could be gained from the material concerned. And, after the period covered in I. Gentles, 'The Struggle for London in the Great Civil War', *Historical Journal* (1983), relatively little is known about the metropolis itself. Furthermore, the only attempt to rationalise what is now known about the localities in the Interregnum is in parts of Anthony Fletcher, *Reform in the Provinces* (1986), which is extremely valuable but only concerned with some aspects of the topic.

The local studies contain much to supplement the works upon aspects of religion and political groupings cited above. They also contain much material upon the question of the disposal of confiscated lands, to which should be added I. Gentles, 'The Sale of Crown Lands during the English Revolution', *Economic History Review* (1973), and 'The Sale of Bishops' Lands in the English Revolution', *English Historical Review* (1980); the debate betwen Gentles and M. Kishlansky in *Economic History Review* (1976); and H. Habbakuk, 'The Parliamentary Army and Crown Lands', *Welsh History Review* (1966–7). There is important unpublished work by Paul Gladwish upon the same topic. The local studies also contain much upon the subject of social relations in the period, alongside which should be set Donald Veall, *The Popular Movement for Law Reform 1640–1660* (1970); A. Beier, 'Poor Relief in Warwickshire 1630–1660', *Past and Present* (1966); J. Walter and K. Wrightson, 'Dearth and the Social Order in Early Modern England', *Past and Present* (1976); J. Morrill and J. Walter, 'Order and Disorder in the English Revolution', in *Order and Disorder in Early Modern England* (ed. by Anthony Fletcher and John Stevenson, 1985); Buchanan Sharp, *In Contempt of All Authority* (1980); Keith Lindley, *Fenland Riots and the English Revolution* (1982); J. Cooper, 'Social and Economic Policies under the Commonwealth', in Aylmer (ed.), *The Interregnum*; G. Ramsay, 'Industrial Laisser-Faire and the Policy of Cromwell', in Roots (ed.), *Cromwell: A Profile*; and Maurice Ashley, *Financial and Commercial Policy under the Cromwellian Protectorate* (3rd edition, 1972); and C. Durston, 'Unhallowed Wedlocks: the Regulation of Marriage during the English Revolution', *Historical Journal* (1988). Dr Durston has a book in the press upon the family during the period. It is another irony of the concentration of research upon local topics that we currently know far more about the operation of local than of central governmental machinery. G. E. Aylmer, *The State's Servants* (1973) is a good study of the people who ran the central machine, but we do need much more information upon the machine itself.

The republic's European diplomacy and its wars with European powers are, again, very imperfectly studied. Additions have been made to our knowledge by Charles Wilson, *Profit and Power* (1964); S. Groenveld, 'The English Civil Wars as a cause of the First Anglo-Dutch War', *Historical Journal* (1987); and J. Israel, 'Competing Cousins', *History Today* (1988). But there is still as yet nothing to replace Gardiner and Firth, cited at the beginning, and Korr's book, cited above, is no more than a spirited introductory essay which has not been followed up.

By contrast, some very recent and first-class research has been published upon Scottish and Irish affairs in the period. Scotland is fairly well covered between David Stevenson, *Revolution and Counter-Revolution in Scotland* (1977); F. D. Dow, *Cromwellian Scotland* (Edinburgh, 1979); and J. Buckroyd, 'Bridging the Gap: Scotland 1659–1660', *Scottish Historical Review* (1987). Ireland after 1653 is excellently served by T. C. Barnard, *Cromwellian Ireland* (Oxford, 1975). The real gap consists of Irish history 1649–53, for which *A New History of Ireland* (ed. by T. W. Moody, F. X. Martin and F. J. Byrne, Oxford, 1978), vol. iii, is helpful but does not really replace Gardiner. We also need a really good biography of Roger Boyle, as that by Kathleen Lynch is too brief and not sufficiently critical of its sources.

It is worth pointing out, in conclusion, that the British Republic has been more, and not less, well covered by historians than most periods and topics. That so much remains to be done is surely a message of hope for future scholars.

INDEX

Index

Index